STUDIES IN ECONOMIC AND SOCIAL HISTORY

This series, specially commissioned by the Economic History Society, provides a guide to the current interpretations of the key themes of economic and social history in which advances have recently been made or in which there has been significant debate.

Originally entitled 'Studies in Economic History', in 1974 the series had its scope extended to include topics in social history, and the new series title, 'Studies in Economic and Social History', signalises this development.

The series gives readers access to the best work done, helps them to draw their own conclusions in major fields of study, and by means of the critical bibliography in each book guides them in the selection of further reading. The aim is to provide a springboard to further work rather than a set of pre-packaged conclusions or short-cuts.

ECONOMIC HISTORY SOCIETY

The Economic History Society, which numbers around 3000 members, publishes the *Economic History Review* four times a year (free to members) and holds an annual conference. Enquiries about membership should be addressed to the Assistant Secretary, Economic History Society, P.O. Box 190, 1 Greville Road, Cambridge, CB1 3QG. Full-time students may join at special rates.

STUDIES IN ECONOMIC AND SOCIAL HISTORY

Edited for the Economic History Society by L.A. Clarkson

PUBLISHED

OTHER TITLES ARE IN PREPARATION

The English Poor Law 1531–1782

Prepared for
the Economic History Society by

PAUL SLACK

Fellow and Tutor in Modern History
Exeter College, Oxford

MACMILLAN

First published 1990 by
THE MACMILLAN PRESS LTD
Houndmills, Basingstoke, Hampshire RG21 2XS
and London
Companies and representatives
throughout the world

ISBN 0–333–34869–9

A catalogue record for this book is available
from the British Library.

Printed in Hong Kong

Reprinted 1992

Contents

Note on References

References in the text in square brackets are detailed in the Select Bibliography. The author's name and date of publication are followed, where necessary, by the page numbers in italics.

The Bibliography is divided into a number of sections to cover different topics of interest. Authors are listed alphabetically within each section.

Editor's Preface

When this series was established in 1968 the first editor, the late Professor M. W. Flinn, laid down three guiding principles. The books should be concerned with important fields of economic history; they should be surveys of the current state of scholarship rather than a vehicle for the specialist views of the authors; and, above all, they were to be introductions to their subject and not 'a set of pre-packaged conclusions'. These aims were admirably fulfilled by Professor Flinn and by his successor, Professor T. C. Smout, who took over the series in 1977. As it passes to its third editor and approaches its third decade, the principles remain the same.

Nevertheless, times change, even though principles do not. The series was launched when the study of economic history was burgeoning and new findings and fresh interpretations were threatening to overwhelm students – and sometimes their teachers. The series has expanded its scope, particularly in the area of social history – although the distinction between 'economic' and 'social' is sometimes hard to recognise and even more difficult to sustain. It has also extended geographically; its roots remain firmly British, but an increasing number of titles is concerned with the economic and social history of the wider world. However, some of the early titles can no longer claim to be introductions to the current state of scholarship; and the discipline as a whole lacks the heady growth of the 1960s and early 1970s. To overcome the first problem a number of new editions, or entirely new works, have been commissioned – some have already appeared. To deal with the second, the aim remains to publish up-to-date introductions to important areas of debate. If the series can demonstrate to students and their teachers the importance of the discipline of economic and social history and excite its further study, it will continue the task so ably begun by its first two editors.

L.A. CLARKSON
Editor

Introduction

The Old Poor Law lies at the intersection of several of the most interesting themes in the history of early modern England. It is related, of course, to economic and social circumstances, to the existence of poverty and destitution which it was designed to treat. It was affected also by social attitudes, not only because poverty is a relative term and perceptions of it change, but also because the poor law was intended to do more than cater for measurable economic need: it had wider aims and certainly wider effects. Finally, it was influenced by the ways in which English government functioned, and it powerfully influenced them in its turn. Recent historical research has thrown light on all these topics. This introductory survey is intended to bring them together in an account of how the poor law came into being and what its impact was.

The chronological limits to this essay have been set by statutes: the first sixteenth century poor law of 1531 and 'Gilbert's Act' of 1782. The discussion will necessarily stray a little beyond these boundaries, but it will not, I hope, trespass too far. I want in particular to avoid as far as possible any implication of purposeful movement towards 1834 and the New Poor Law, such as might arise if the story were extended into the 1790s. As will appear, it is not possible entirely to avoid that Whiggish perspective: discussion of reform in the 1780s anticipated much that followed as well as reflecting the past. But what followed has in any case been treated in another work in this series, and the secondary literature on it is enormous [Marshall, 1968/1985].

Unfortunately, the same cannot be said about the period before I begin. The character of late medieval social welfare is still in many respects obscure. But I have chosen to start in 1531 because my subject is the poor *law*, its development and its consequences. However much it may simply have applied new mechanisms to activities formerly conducted in other ways, those mechanisms mattered: they shaped and changed the purposes to which they were put. Much more has been written on these matters by historians of the later sixteenth and seventeenth centuries than by historians of the eighteenth, although there are now signs that the balance is being redressed.[1] One purpose of this essay has hence been to carry a relatively well-documented story forward beyond 1700, and to raise questions where historical research has yet to provide us with answers.

The discussion has been organised in four chapters, all of them overlapping chronologically to some degree, but considering different themes. The first looks at the shaping of the law to 1601, and the role of economic circumstances, intellectual and social attitudes and political institutions in that process. The second surveys the ways in which the law was implemented, chiefly in the seventeenth century, and the amounts of money raised for the relief of the poor down to the 1780s. The third chapter discusses the methods adopted in an attempt to cut costs from the 1660s onwards. Some broader questions are then considered in Chapter 4: the relationship between public poor relief and private charity; their impact on poverty itself; and the implications of the whole story for English government. These topics return us to the triad of influences – intellectual, economic and social, and political – which were introduced in Chapter 1, and which gave muscle and vigour to the law. The Appendix is a reminder of the firmness of the statutory skeleton and, I hope, a useful chronological guide: it summarises the long sequence of enactments whose origins and consequences this essay sets out to explore.

1 Defining Strategies

'The kingdom became then much more populous than in former times, and with it the poor also greatly increased.' That was part of the explanation for the Elizabethan poor law put forward in the mid-seventeenth century by Sir Matthew Hale.[2] It has had echoes in later interpretations, and it is one of the three possible approaches to our subject. We might call it the 'high-pressure' interpretation. According to this, poor laws were stimulated by economic circumstances, and particularly by population pressure. The second interpretation looks instead to changes in public attitudes: the crucial factor was a new conception of what governments could and should do for the poor, inspired by humanism, Protestantism or Puritanism (the choice varies between historians). Thirdly, some would stress government itself: the political ambitions of central government, Parliament or local elites (again the emphasis varies), who wished to control their subjects and inferiors. We need to take all three approaches into account, though none of them is quite as straightforward as it first seems.

(i) CIRCUMSTANCES

To an extent, Hale was right. The legislation of 1598 and 1601 was passed at a time when the problem of poverty was unusually severe. The harvests of 1596 and 1597 were among the worst of the period, and the medium-term economic trend was adverse. The population of England had been increasing since at least the 1520s, possibly since the 1470s, and so had prices. Food supplies and employment opportunities did not keep pace. So far as we can tell, the real value of wages fell to its lowest point in the

11

years around 1630; and the consequences were certainly evident for half a century before then. This was the period during which illegitimacy rates rose to a peak, and probably levels of crime and vagrancy also [Slack, 1988, *102–3*; Beier, 1985]. It is not difficult to see why poverty seemed a threat and improved policing a necessary response in the later sixteenth and early seventeenth centuries.

Another response was a broadening of contemporary definitions of poverty. Alongside the 'impotent' poor, the widows and orphans traditionally regarded as meriting charity, there were now frequent references to labouring householders who did not earn enough to support their children. The term 'labouring poor' seems to have been coined by Daniel Defoe in *The True Born Englishman* (1701). But the concept and the reality date back to the earlier period of demographic growth. They can be found in listings of those who required relief during the bad harvests of the 1590s and early 1620s – people categorised as 'poor able labouring folk' or 'labouring persons not able to live off their labour'; in a survey of the poor in London in 1552 which uncovered numbers of 'decayed householders' and 'poor men overburdened with their children' [Slack, 1988, *27–9*]; and, first of all, in the monastic visitation injunctions of 1535–6 which referred to 'those which endeavour themselves with all their will and labour to get their living with their hands, and yet cannot fully help themselves for their chargeable household and multitude of children'.[3]

The high-pressure interpretation thus has a good deal to be said for it as an explanation of why poverty and new categories of pauper should engage attention in the latter part of the sixteenth century. But it also has limitations. First, it has the obvious disadvantage of failing to explain concern about the poor in 'low-pressure' periods: between 1660 and 1760, for example, when we shall see that the poor-relief machine continued, not simply to function, but to expand. It might be argued that the proportion of the population dependent on wages and therefore at the mercy of market fluctuations continued to increase after 1660, and that that constituted a mounting problem [Slack, 1988, *45–7*]. But it might equally be argued that demands for labour discipline and attacks on idleness were stimulated then, not by labour surpluses and declining real wages, but by their opposite:

12

by conditions of relative labour shortage and rising popular living standards.

Similar problems arise if we consider the later Middle Ages. Although there was then no elaborate state-regulated provision for the poor, there was discrimination between those deserving and not deserving relief; there were institutions – hospitals, alms-houses – for the destitute; and there was a system of parochial or communal support [Tierney, 1959]. Part of the concern about the poor in the later fifteenth century may be attributable to the beginnings of population growth and migration. There is again an alternative argument, however: that it was economic depression and a scarcity of resources in the later Middle Ages which turned attention to the need for discrimination [McIntosh, 1988; Rubin, 1987, 50–3, 290–9]. That conflict cannot be resolved here. But if low and high pressure, labour scarcity and labour surplus, may equally provoke calls for regulation, then economic circumstances can do little to help us explain innovations in social policy.

There is a second difficulty with the 'high-pressure' interpretation of English reactions to poverty: namely, the fact that the pressure in England was never as great as in some other countries. Early modern Englishmen thought that they were better-off than Frenchmen, for example, and they were right. There is clear evidence of malnutrition in the most impoverished parts of England on occasions when the harvest failed between 1520 and 1630, particularly in 1586–7, 1597–8 and 1622–3 [Appleby, 1978]; but there was not the mass starvation which afflicted France. Yet only England produced a system of poor relief financed by taxation. This may be to say no more than that *absolute* levels of poverty are less important than perceptions of *relative* deprivation: but that itself turns our attention away from circumstances, and gives attitudes as great an importance as economic realities.

Finally, it may be argued that certain permanent features of economic and social circumstances were more important than short-term fluctuations. The general recognition that the community rather than the family ought to support its poorer members was not new in the sixteenth century. It had long been a necessary consequence of a social structure in which the dominance of the nuclear family and the formation of separate households at marriage meant that the elderly required communal support; and people over 60 were never less than 7 per cent of the total population. Disease and disability were similarly constant causes of dependence: they might push a similar proportion of the population into poverty [Smith, 1984; Thomson, 1986; Pelling, 1988]. It needs to be stressed that public assistance under the poor law was intended for these 'impotent' persons – the poor who were always there; and although short-term crises or periods of high pressure might necessarily increase the number claiming relief, there was no shortage of claimants at other times. The question was not whether collective assistance should be provided for these people, but who should assist them and in what ways.

(ii) ASPIRATIONS

Before 1500 that assistance had been provided by a miscellany of means: religious institutions – monasteries, fraternities and gilds; or village and parish resources – town 'stocks', almshouses, church collections. There had been no co-ordination and little activity by the state, aside from legislation regulating labour and punishing beggars and vagrants [Tierney, 1959; Wright, 1988, 29–84]. After 1530, however, there was increasing government interference, centralisation and uniformity.

The intellectual roots of the change did not lie initially in Protestantism, as some historians once argued [Jordan, 1959]. For change had begun before Protestantism was firmly established, and it was visible in Catholic countries as well as in those which became Protestant. Intervention by lay authorities, centralisation and the establishment of new institutions for poor relief can be found all over western Europe from the 1520s to the 1560s, in Catholic towns such as Lyons and Venice, as well as in Protestant Strasbourg or Geneva [Lis and Soly, 1979; Pullan, 1976]. Their common inspiration was humanism: the Christian humanism of Erasmus and Juan Luis Vives, whose writings on poverty were particularly influential.

Humanist attitudes towards social welfare had three elements which – in different combinations – continued to influence social policy throughout our period. First, there was Christian charity, the traditional obligations of the rich towards the poor, but it

14

should be directed to particular rational ends, not indulged in simply for the salvation or self-satisfaction of the donor. Secondly, the aim should be reform, and particularly moral reform. This was also an old theme, familiar in medieval sermons against idleness; but it was reinforced by what appears to be a new revulsion against the dirt and disease as well as indiscipline of the poor, a fear of contamination which runs through much of the contemporary literature. Finally, reform should be carried out by public authority, and it should be thorough. Governments not only had a duty to engage in social engineering, but engineering was possible. There was a new optimism about what government could achieve and that included the elimination of poverty [Todd, 1987, *118–47*].

We can see all these ingredients in operation in the England of Henry VIII and Edward VI. New fashions in government were not lost on Cardinal Wolsey. He instigated a campaign against vagrants and beggars in 1517, alongside the famous enclosure commission of the same year. In 1518 he set out to copy other states which were trying to control the spread of plague: infected houses in London and Oxford were to be marked so that contagion might be avoided. In 1527 he tackled that other cause of crisis in the commonwealth – dearth: local commissions were to survey stocks of grain and arrange the regular provision of markets. Later governments built on these beginnings, as we shall see, but the cardinal can claim to be the founder of Tudor paternalism [Slack, 1988, *116–17*].

At the same time, English writers were echoing humanist themes and providing propaganda for government interference. In the 1530s William Marshall was horrified by the 'divers diseases, contagions and infirmities' and the 'heinous deeds, detestable sins, crimes and offences' of the poor. Thomas Starkey thought the 'multitude of beggars here in our country showeth much poverty... and ... also much idleness and ill policy'. Such criticisms were the background to the poor laws of 1531 and 1536 which we will consider in a moment. They were the setting also for a remodelling of social welfare in London, which gave mid-Tudor England a centre of civic reform comparable to those in Germany and France [Slack, 1988, *23*, *116*, *119–21*].

Between 1544 and 1557 the rulers of London established a

coherent system of hospitals to cater for the different categories of pauper in the capital: St Bartholomew's and St Thomas's for the diseased and disabled, Christ's Hospital and Bridewell for foundling children and idle rogues. All these should be taken off the streets, away from the 'dunghills' which bred vice and contagion, and cured wherever possible, whether by medical care or by training, work and discipline. Christian charity dictated no less – 'Christ should lie no more abroad in the streets', urged Bishop Ridley – and charity (along with a temporary tax on the citizens) would ensure funding for the scheme. All should be controlled at the centre by a board of governors. The aspirations and the mechanisms were comparable to those in other European cities at the time. The centralising impetus was weakened later, undercut by the parish poor relief sanctioned by Elizabethan statutes; but the London hospitals themselves survived – reminders that English responses to poverty had in origin been part of a European movement.

It has already been said that that movement was humanist rather than Protestant in inspiration. Catholic as well as Protestant aldermen were active in the London scheme. Yet the Reformation cannot be left out of the story: on the contrary, it had two important effects. First, it made civic or government interference with religious and charitable institutions easier than it would otherwise have been. It is significant that the London hospitals were hampered by government suspicion in Mary's reign, because they occupied ecclesiastical property and trespassed on the jurisdiction of ecclesiastical courts. [Cf. Todd, 1987, 246–7] Secondly, the Reformation destroyed much of the institutional fabric which had provided charity for the poor in the past: monasteries, gilds and fraternities. Their dissolution in 1538 and 1547 left a perceived vacuum which had somehow to be filled.

The dissolution also limited the ways in which the vacuum could be filled. Attacks on poverty could not be mounted through religious orders and fraternities, as they were in Catholic countries. Sir Martin Bowes, one of the prime movers behind the London hospitals, had planned a 'brotherhood of the poor', a charitable fraternity of the rich and benevolent; it had no future after 1547, and such cooperative endeavours by groups of

16

private individuals were indeed remarkable by their absence from English philanthropy until the later seventeenth century. Nevertheless, many options remained open. Poverty might have been dealt with by scores of workhouses and almshouses, as it was in the Low Countries, or by major institutions, general hospitals of the kind erected in French cities and begun in London. All these existed in England. But they were not the dominant feature of English poor relief by 1601. That place was occupied by parish rates and parish doles, by local taxes and cash payments to many hundreds of paupers living at home. Neither economic and social circumstances nor humanism and Protestantism explain why this was so. We must look for an answer in the legislative process.

(iii) THE LAW

If Wolsey was the founder of Tudor paternalism, Thomas Cromwell gave it its statutory expression. The first Tudor poor laws of 1495 and 1531 were largely concerned with ways of punishing vagrants and sending them home, though the second added that deserving paupers could be licensed to beg. Thomas Cromwell's statute of 1536 went much further. The original bill, probably based on a scheme by William Marshall, provided for public works for vagabonds and even perhaps an income tax to finance them. It would have given a directing hand to a central 'council', and it proved too much for the Reformation Parliament. But the final Act, leaving power in local hands, was radical enough. Vagabonds were to be set to work when they arrived home and poor children put out to service. As for the impotent poor, weekly collections should be organised for them in every parish, and indiscriminate almsgiving banned. Though undermined by a series of provisos added by Parliament, the intention was plainly to control all charitable giving through a 'common box' in every parish [Elton, 1974].

The statute lapsed soon after it was passed, but it defined the strategy for the future: work as well as punishment for the idle and able-bodied poor; cash payments to those who could not work; and, as a consequence, a ban on begging and casual almsgiving. It was notable also in placing responsibility for relieving the impotent in the hands of parish officers. Parish collections for the poor were common, though not required by law, before 1536; and charitable activities, of fraternities, for example, had sometimes had a parochial base. It was natural to recognise the parish as the unit of administration. But in doing this the 1536 Act marked a shift of emphasis away from hundreds, manors and courts leet, which were alternative units for social regulation, and began the construction of the 'civil parish' [McIntosh, 1988, *224–30*; Wright, 1988, *77*].

Progress was slow after 1536. An Act of 1547, imposing two years of slavery on vagabonds, proved impractical and a false turn [Davies, 1966]. It contained clauses about the employment of poor children and collections for the impotent, however, and these survived and were substantially built upon in 1552. There were now to be surveys of the poor in every parish, so that the needs of the impotent might be precisely measured, and records of the amounts parishioners agreed to contribute weekly to their support. The initial bill discussed in 1552, but not passed, may even have provided for compulsory taxation. A statute of 1563 hinted at it again: those refusing to contribute to the poor could be bound over to appear before the justices. Finally, a comprehensive poor law of 1572 went the whole way. Justices of the peace were to take surveys of the poor and then to 'tax and assess' all the inhabitants to provide for them, appointing collectors and overseers to handle the money. There were also clauses punishing vagrants and providing work for them; and these were supported in 1576 by the introduction of stocks of materials on which the poor should be employed and county houses of correction for the incarceration of the incorrigible. The agenda mapped out in 1536 had been largely completed.

What remained was the need to make its enforcement more practicable, and that was the achievement of the famous statutes of 1598 and 1601 which defined the Old Poor Law once and for all. The Vagrancy Act of 1598 simplified penalties and procedures: parish officers could whip vagabonds and return them home; there was no need for quarter sessions to deal with every case, as in 1572. The 1598 Act for the Relief of the Poor, substantially repeated in 1601, had a similar purpose. The burden of raising rates, relieving the impotent, setting the able-bodied to work and apprenticing poor children, was placed firmly on the shoulders of churchwardens and overseers of the poor in every parish. Justices of the peace were only to exercise a supervisory role, including hearing appeals against parish decisions.

Other pieces of legislation at this time give the impression of loose ends being tied up in the interests of implementing a relatively coherent strategy. Two Acts of 1598 prescribed the treatment of maimed, idle and disorderly soldiers returning from the wars. Two others attacked the more complex but equally familiar problem of endowed charities. One set out to make the founding of almshouses and hospitals easier; the other provided mechanisms for investigating breaches of charitable trusts, and was elaborated in the Charitable Uses Act of 1601. The process of accretion and clarification did not stop in 1603. In 1610 a statute resolved doubts about the legality of the summary imprisonment of 'idle and disorderly persons' in houses of correction. In all essentials, however, the poor law was complete in 1601 [Slack, 1988, *122–31*].

It had been a long time in the making, and much remains obscure in its genesis. What is clear is that several interests and pressures came together in the legislative process; what is not clear is how precisely they were balanced. The central government plainly had a voice, whether that of the Council or of individual councillors. It pushed for legislation in 1536 and in 1572 and 1576; and its concern was usually with public order, and hence with vagrancy, particularly after the rising in the North in 1569 and after an abortive rising in Oxfordshire in 1596. Ordinary MPs shared the same worries, but some of them also contributed knowledge of local experiments in poor relief which might be models for general adoption. There were compulsory taxes for the poor in London, Norwich, York, Colchester, Ipswich and Cambridge between 1547 and 1557, in advance of the 1572 statute; and Bridewells, make-work schemes and censuses of the poor were increasingly common in mid century.

Any particular statute might therefore have several authors. Martin Bowes, alderman of London, sat in the Commons in 1552 and 1555, but we do not know whether or how much he contributed to the poor laws of those years. Much the same applies to John Aldrich, MP in 1572 and 1576, and mayor of

Norwich in 1570 when poor relief was reformed in ways which seem to anticipate the statutes of the 1570s. In 1563 the bishops may have been behind poor-relief legislation, and in 1598 a group of Puritan members was active in pushing for 'reformation', in social welfare as elsewhere. In short, several interests were in negotiation and contributed to the result. There were often several bills on poor relief in a session, as in 1547, 1552, 1571–2 and 1598, before a final Act emerged, and there were committees to review the existing laws and consider new ones in 1593 and 1598 [Slack, 1988, *122–6*; Elton, 1986, *268–9, 271*].

Obscure though its details are, this complicated parliamentary history is of major importance for our subject. It determined what the poor law was and what it could not be. It could not be an ambitious blueprint for social reconstruction founded on discriminatory institutions like the London hospitals, or major schemes for public works financed by central taxation like those conceived in 1536, or a new kind of slavery as in 1547. Such utopian ideals were cut down to size by the realities of local government represented in Parliament by sceptical MPs. The poor law had to be applicable to small rural communities as well as major cities. It was likely to reflect the interests of those who had traditionally managed charitable distributions alongside the religious institutions and fraternities destroyed at the Reformation. It was bound, therefore, to be parochial if it was to be nationally uniform – paradoxical as that might seem. It was bound also to be, in practice if not always in intention, permissive and discretionary. Such matters as who was to be counted a vagrant (a topic much disputed in the Commons in 1571 and 1572) had in the end to be left to local constables and justices to determine; similarly the question of who were the impotent. Work-stocks might not always seem appropriate in villages or workhouses worth the trouble they caused in towns. As we shall see, the implementation of the law shaped its character, and the lowest common denominator of what was acceptable triumphed.

Yet the long process of parliamentary debate and successive enactments had ensured that the lowest common denominator was not negligible. It is not surprising that one element – police activity against the rogue and vagabond – appealed to all in authority both centrally and locally. But the other – a local tax for the poor – was a much more striking achievement, and one unique to England. It could scarcely have been brought about without the new circumstances and new perceptions (particularly of the vacuum left by the Reformation) which were mentioned earlier. It could not have been achieved in a state less used to central direction than that of Tudor England. But it would probably not have been achieved either if control of that tax had not been left in local hands for local purposes. We shall see that that posed problems for the future, but it was a condition implicit in the consultative processes which had put the Elizabethan poor laws on the statute book in the first place.

2 Implementing the Law

The implementation of the poor law depended upon a combination of forces as complex as its creation. Continuing direction from the centre, at least until 1630, further contributions from committed activists in the localities, and the slower response of parish officers conspired to produce the national welfare system which the poor law had become by 1700. Elizabethan legislators would have welcomed its uniformity. They could not have predicted its cost.

(i) DIRECTION AND EXPERIMENT

The push from the centre, transmitted by proclamations, lists of articles and circular letters, largely and predictably related to public order and crisis-management. The Elizabethan Privy Council invented printed 'Books of Orders', one dealing with outbreaks of plague in 1578, and another with bad harvests in 1586. Building on the policies begun by Wolsey in 1518 and 1527, they told justices of the peace what to do in these emergencies: quarantine and relieve the sick; survey grain stocks and regulate their sale to the poor. Reissued whenever epidemics or dearth recurred, the books rested solely on the royal prerogative, and to that extent they were not strictly part of the poor *law*, at least until a statute of 1604 authorising action against plague. Like the Jacobean articles regulating alehouses, however, their general concern with the management and relief of the poor undoubtedly reinforced the message of the statutes of 1572 and 1598. They also provided the model for the famous Caroline Book of Orders: the *Orders and Directions* of January 1631, which proclaimed the social policy of Charles I's period of personal rule.

Too much significance has sometimes been attributed to this publication because it has been seen in isolation. Its 'directions' rehearsed familiar items of social policy. Its 'orders' prescribed administrative arrangements like the regular 'divisional' meetings of local justices of the peace which were already taking place in some counties. The book's author, Henry Montagu, Earl of Manchester, certainly drew on the experience of his brother, a Northamptonshire justice, as well as on his own attempts as Lord Chief Justice to improve local administration, or 'quicken' it, as he liked to say. The only novelties in the Book, and the reasons for its unpopularity, were the commission of Privy Councillors appointed to supervise its implementation and the provision for regular reports from the counties on what had been done. Unpopular or not, many counties obeyed. Nearly one thousand reports came in in the course of the 1630s, telling the Council what it wanted to hear: the number of vagrants punished, alehouses closed down and poor children bound as apprentices [Slack, 1980; Quintrell, 1980].

These were probably local priorities in any case. Justices already knew the law. For more than a generation they had had printed handbooks describing what it was and how it should be enforced. Their manuscripts show that they copied them out and followed them to the letter. They scarcely needed telling in the half-century before 1640 that poverty was dangerous. Parish lists of vagrants punished, county appointments of provost marshals for the same purpose, and the number of Bridewells and houses of correction (more than one hundred by 1630) testify to their response [Clark and Souden, 1987, 49–76; Innes, 1987, 62]. The collapse of Charles I's personal rule in 1640, which ended central direction for good, did not therefore lead to the collapse of social policy, as was once thought. Justices were no less active after 1640 in the tasks they had learnt since 1598: quite the contrary [Leonard, 1900, 268; Beier, 1966]. It follows that the course taken by the poor law at the local level might have been much the same even without conciliar direction. Circular letters, Books of Orders and energetic judges on circuit probably accelerated the process, 'quickened' it in a literal sense. It would be impossible to argue, counterfactually, that the process would not have occurred without them.

23

The same conclusion might be reached about some of the ambitious local experiments in social welfare which were erected on the statutory foundation of the poor law. They occurred chiefly in corporate towns, and – in the period from 1570 to the 1630s – in municipalities ruled by Puritans. In Norwich and other East Anglian towns in the 1570s, in Salisbury, Dorchester and other western towns in the 1620s, alliances of godly magistrates and ministers sought to remodel their little commonwealths, and they used the management of the poor as a tool for that purpose. If idleness were rooted out, drunkards, bastard-bearers, hedge-breakers and other rogues would disappear. Poverty itself might be conquered along with ungodliness, if only there were sufficient investment in social engineering. Accordingly, there were censuses and listings of the poor, workhouses and schooling for poor children, storehouses and hospitals, municipal enterprises such as the breweries of Dorchester and Salisbury whose profits went to the poor, and – for a time – larger pensions to more paupers [Slack, 1988, *148–56*; Beier, 1981; Pound, 1962; Slack, 1972].

The application of the epithet 'Puritan' to such experiments has been questioned by some historians. It has been pointed out that their ingredients were not new: the objectives and the solutions were the common property of humanists, in England and abroad, before Puritans were ever heard of [Todd, 1987]. It might be argued also that their character was largely determined by the pressure of circumstances, by population growth and hard times, which occurred at other times with somewhat similar results - in the thirteenth century or the later eighteenth century, for example: the conjunction of innovations in social welfare and Puritan enthusiasm might be coincidence, not effect and cause.[4] Both arguments are weighty. These municipal experiments plainly owed a good deal to the example of the London hospitals. It is difficult also to find a town beset with a declining textile industry and increasing unemployment between 1570 and 1640 which did not, to some degree, engage in novel schemes for the regulation and relief of the poor. Yet it is equally difficult to find a municipal scheme unsupported by Puritan or godly rhetoric. Puritanism did not 'cause' welfare reform;

but the two flourished and interacted in the same social and civic circumstances. The quest for godly reformation was more than a new cloak for old aspirations. For men like John Ivie, mayor of Salisbury, or John White, minister of Dorchester, it was the indispensable driving force for their realisation.

It continued to be influential after the 1630s. It can be found in the pamphlet literature on poverty of the Interregnum and in the projects, often by Dissenters, of the 1660s and 1670s, which sometimes referred back to earlier municipal enterprises. It inspired the London Corporation of the Poor, established by parliamentary ordinances of 1647 and 1649, which centralised control of poor relief in the parishes of the city, trained eighty or so children in workhouses, and set to work a thousand other poor elsewhere [Webster, 1975; Appleby, 1978, *129–57*; Pearl, 1978]. As we shall see, that in turn was a model for corporations in other towns at the end of the seventeenth century.

Persistent as they were, however, all these projects failed in the end, for a variety of reasons. The London Corporation fell at the Restoration, and other schemes collapsed with the political fortunes of the sectional interests which supported them. Financially, they all involved expensive outlay on new institutions such as workhouses and continuing heavy overheads which could never be recouped. Politically, their centralising impetus ran into the opposition of parish authorities, jealous of their discretionary powers to determine who should be relieved and how, and able to ally with factions in civic elites opposing the troublesome innovations of godly magistrates. This at least was the political line-up in Salisbury, and its outlines can be traced elsewhere, from Elizabethan Warwick to later Stuart London [Slack, 1972; Beier, 1981; Macfarlane, 1986]. In short, energetic innovation cost too much and offended too many vested interests to be successful in the longer term. Like conciliar direction it could accelerate the implementation of the law; but in the last resort, in most places, the responsibility for poor relief lay in the hands of churchwardens, overseers and vestries in the 9000 parishes of England and Wales.

(ii) THE PARISH

The slow, insidious but crucially formative development of parish poor relief is more difficult to map than the more spectacular, and temporary, achievements of Privy Councillors and Puritan magistrates. The sources are scattered, where they survive at all, and have still to be properly exploited. By 1600 most of the larger towns seem to have had poor rates, as we would expect from what has already been said, but only a small minority of rural parishes, most of them probably in the south-east [cf. Emmison, 1931; 1953]. In some places rating was tried only for a year or two; in others it was said to be unnecessary; many parishes did nothing. The decisive move towards the widespread implementation of the law came only after 1601, helped by pressure from the centre, through Assize judges lecturing magistrates who in turn used constables to stir a parish response [Fletcher, 1986, *213–16*; Kent, 1986, *29–30, 188*]. There seems to have been particular activity in 1618 and 1619, part of that process of 'quickening' local government which formed the background to the Book of Orders of 1631.[5] It was a slow process, but by 1660 at least a third of parishes were probably well accustomed to raising rates.

In the forty years before 1660 poor rates became familiar. In the next forty years they became universal, at least in England. (Wales did not catch up before the end of the eighteenth century [Dodd, 1926].) In 1696 the Board of Trade set out to discover how much they raised *in toto*. Local surveys were instituted, and the returns for Shropshire and the diocese of Worcester reveal that very few parishes indeed were without a tax for the poor by then.[6] There was heavy expenditure, relative to population, in towns and industrial areas, suggesting that they had been first in the field, but other parishes were copying them. In the end the Board received information from 4415 parishes, and though these were rather less than half the total, it made allowance for omissions and concluded that rates raised £400,000 per annum in England and Wales. It was a rough and ready calculation, but there is no reason to suppose it was an overestimate, and the Board was right to think it a remarkable total [Slack, 1988, *170–1*].

The money was put to a variety of local purposes. It could be used defensively, to avoid future expense: to bind poor children as apprentices, remove pregnant strangers, or even buy housing for native paupers somewhere else. It could be employed to give benefits in kind as well as in cash: shirts, shoes, or lodging; bread or fuel (the latter more commonly than the former by the end of the seventeenth century); medical aid – bone-setting in the seventeenth century, inoculation often in the eighteenth [Pelling, 1985; Thomas, 1980]. It ought to have been used, under the statutes, to provide work, and sometimes was: some parishes had stocks of flax or wool which the poor could spin, and bought spinning wheels or other tools for the able-bodied [Melling, 1964, *16–17, 113*; Webb, 1966, *130–1*].

Any set of overseers' accounts will show, however, that the commonest as well as the easiest form of poor relief was the cash dole. By far the greater part of the £400,000 which was being raised by 1696 must have gone directly to the poor in small weekly sums for 'outdoor relief'. These payments were essentially of two kinds. Some paupers received a weekly pension, agreed once a year, usually at Easter. Others were granted relief for shorter periods of time, when ill or unemployed or simply 'poor': these were termed 'casual', 'extraordinary', or 'discretionary' payments. In general overseers tried to confine regular payments to the impotent: pensioners were usually the old, especially widows, and occasionally women or children, if somehow disabled. Casual payments, by contrast, more often went to able-bodied men. The labouring poor may sometimes have benefited indirectly from pensions formally recorded as going to their children; and they swelled the list of pensioners in some parishes when times were particularly bad. But economic crises generally show themselves in a large number of 'extraordinary' payments, amounting *in toto* to as much as all pensions, in the 1590s and 1690s, for example, or in 1728 and 1741.

Doles varied from person to person as well as from year to year. Overseers' accounts often suggest that there was a going rate: sixpence (6d.) a week was common in the early seventeenth century, a shilling a week by the 1660s. There were endless variations, however, depending as much on social status and moral worth as on need. Widows usually received more than the average; so did people once of respectable status now fallen on hard times. On the other hand, payments to male labourers were often clearly supplementary, intended to make up inadequate earnings. Overseers had considerable discretion in their use of the financial resources, powers of patronage, and opportunities for what we would now call 'social control', that the poor law gave them [Slack, 1988, *173–82*].

They were not totally unsupervised in the exercise of that discretion. After 1598 two justices of the peace were supposed to approve the appointment of overseers and take their accounts. The parish vestry – the voice of the ratepayers – might also have been expected to exercise a restraining hand, at its Easter meeting if not throughout the year. We know very little about the activities of vestries and justices out of sessions, but there is scarcely a hint of restraint. Magistrates, in pairs or in their divisions or petty sessions, ensured that the law was enforced, not ignored [Landau, 1984, *27–8, 216–18*]. They settled rating disputes between and within parishes, and gave orders for the relief of individuals.[7] Quarter sessions not infrequently intervened for the same purpose. Vestries also had business to do: approving rates, hearing petitions, ordering casual relief. One sign of increasing bureaucracy was the advent of small 'close' committees for poor-relief business in 'open' vestries attended by most ratepayers [Hinton, 1940–2, *215*]. Another was the introduction from the later seventeenth century of a standard method of rating: the 'pound rate' assessed on the value of property occupied in a parish. It had the disadvantage of leaving wealth not held in real property untaxed, but it was a convenient device for busy local officials.

The burdens and pressures on an overseer are well revealed in the diary of Thomas Turner of East Hoathly, Sussex, who served for four years in the office in the mid-eighteenth century. He had to pay out doles, deal with vagrants and settlement cases, keep bills and vouchers, and get his accounts approved by justices and his pensions by the vestry. He seems to have been extraordinarily conscientious. Yet he still had to appear before a justice to show why he had refused someone relief, and to defend the parish against the charge of being 'hard to our poor' [Vaisey, 1984, *91–2*]. There must have been many overseers like Turner in the century from 1650 to 1750: men aware of their powers and responsibilities under the law, who knew full well that their neighbours and betters would intervene if they did not exercise them. Poor relief had become a parish business.

That had several results. It meant that far from being impersonal, a business run at a distance according to narrow principles, the relief of the poor was a matter for face-to-face management by overseers among their neighbours. It also meant that expectations were created. It was assumed, by magistrates, managers and the poor themselves, that the poor were entitled to relief if they required it [Slack, 1988, *191–2*]. Since poverty is a relative concept, and it was not difficult to find objects for relief once one looked for them, costs rose.

(iii) RISING COSTS

From what has been said already, we can conclude that the pressures which created rising expenditure came from three directions. First, on the supply side, as it were, the introduction of rates in parishes which had not formerly had them, pushed up aggregate totals. This factor had already done most of its work by the 1690s, except in Wales (which added little to national totals). More continuous were two influences on what we might call the demand side. First there were rising expectations of what the welfare system might accomplish and whom it might relieve. Secondly, there were changes in real circumstances which might in the short or medium term increase the number of those claiming relief: changes in the age structure of the population which might boost the number of elderly pensioners, for example, short-term economic crises pushing up extraordinary expenditure, or overall demographic increase unmatched by an expansion in employment opportunities.

These various 'demand-side' factors might be expected to operate in different ways in different places and at different times. In theory, when economic or demographic circumstances improved, they might have led to a reduction in costs: and although we know much less than we should like about variations in local rates in the eighteenth century, it is clear that they did sometimes fall.

Table 1   Annual Expenditure on Poor Relief in England and Wales 1696–1803

	1	2	3	4	5
	Total expenditure (£s)	Expenditure per head of pop. (shillings)	Expenditure per head (qtrs of wheat)	Potential proportion of pop. relieved (per cent)	Expenditure as per cent of national income
Date					
1696	400,000	1.5	0.04	3.6	0.8
1748–50 (average)	689,971	2.3	0.08	7.9	1.0
1776	1,529,780	4.4	0.10	9.8	1.6
1783–5 (average)	2,004,238	5.3	0.11	10.9	2.0
1802–3	4,267,965	9.5	0.15	14.7	1.9

Sources: Expenditure: Webbs [1927, *153–4*]; population: taken to be (in millions) 5.5, 6.0, 7.0, 7.5 and 9.0 at the successive dates; national income: P.K. O'Brien, 'The political economy of British taxation, 1660–1815', *Economic History Review*, 2nd ser., 41 (1988), 3; wheat prices: the averages for 1694–6, 1748–50, 1775–6, 1783–5 and 1802–3, from W.G. Hoskins, 'Harvest Fluctuations and English Economic History 1620–1759', *Agricultural History Review*, 16 (1968), 30–1, and B.R. Mitchell and P. Deane, *Abstract of British Historical Statistics* (Cambridge, 1971), p. 488. Column 4 is based on the assumption that one quarter of wheat would feed one person for a year.

But local reductions seem always to have been outweighed by increasing expenditure elsewhere, so that the gross national total was always rising, as Table 1 suggests. Column 1 gives the only contemporary estimates of relief expenditure in which we can place much confidence. The Board of Trade's calculation for 1696, though based on extrapolation from partial returns, seems likely to be closer to the truth than other, higher, figures sometimes given for the later seventeenth century. The totals for the years 1748–50, 1776 and 1783–5 come from parliamentary inquiries which were more complete, as does the figure for 1802–3 which is added to indicate the trend after the end of our period. These are, of course, only individual years, and some of them may have been untypical. In particular, expenditure on the poor may have been unusually high both in 1783–5 and in 1802–3. The trend suggested by the table seems clear enough, however, even if we cannot assume that it described a straight line between the years for which we have data.

In simple cash terms (column 1), the rise in costs is particularly notable in the second half of the eighteenth century. The total more than doubled between 1750 and 1776, rose by a further quarter to 1785 and then doubled again by 1802. Even if we take into account population growth, the rise was greater in the second half of the century. As the second column shows, expenditure per head of population rose by half down to 1750 but more than doubled between then and 1785. If we also adjust for price changes, however, the rate of growth of expenditure appears more even. Column 3 shows expenditure per head in terms of the amount of wheat it would buy. That doubled between 1696 and 1750 and nearly doubled again between 1750 and 1803. Rising prices and rising population vastly inflated total cash payments after 1750, but in real per capita terms they grew relatively steadily over the whole period from 1696 to 1803, though slowing a little between 1750 and 1785 and then accelerating.

The same data can be reworked to indicate, again in real terms, the quantity of relief that could be purchased at the various dates. It was generally accepted by contemporaries that one quarter of wheat would feed an adult for a year. Hence we can calculate the figures in column 4: the proportion of the total population that could be supported in food throughout the year from poor-relief expenditure. The numbers naturally suggest the same steady growth, from less than 4 per cent in 1696 to about 11 per cent in 1785. It should be stressed that these proportions are artificial. Since many people had relief which supplemented their earnings or supported them for less than twelve months, they are minima. It is important to note also that the 'real' calculations in columns 3 and 4 are extremely sensitive to variations in wheat prices. Prices were high in 1692–6, for example. If the level of relief stayed much the same in cash terms after 1696, it would then support more people: 4.8 per cent of the population in fact in 1700. It is highly probable that poor rates were less elastic than wheat prices, and that complicates measurement of how their purchasing power changed over time.

The figures in columns 3 and 4 do, however, have one important salutary effect. They direct our attention to the period before 1750, which has been neglected by historians mesmerised by the cash totals and public debates of the later eighteenth century. Between 1696 and 1750 expenditure on the poor doubled in real terms, and that needs to be explained. It is really a problem pertaining to the whole period from 1660 to 1750, when prices and population were generally stable, but poor-relief costs grew. The spread of rates to parishes which had not formerly had them may help to account for this before 1696, but not after that date. Another kind of 'catching-up' operation may have been more continuous: the value of individual pensions was probably rising to the point where they met most, and not just a small part, of the living expenses of those on the dole – replacing income from begging and informal charity. Although this seems to have occurred in some parts of the country in the years before 1696, others may have caught up later. The evidence is fragmentary, and what there is points in different directions [Slack, 1988, *189*; Wales, 1984, *356*; Ashby, 1912, *115*; Edmonds, 1966, *6*; Emmison, 1933, *12*; Ripley, 1985, *192*, *193*, *197*].

Surprising as it may seem, given the economic background, the number of pensioners may also have been rising, though less rapidly than the value of pensions. There were economic dislocations and crises between the 1690s and 1720s which must have increased the demand for relief from the able-bodied: it is well documented in the case of Norwich. Such crises were temporary, but the increases in rates levied to meet them were not always followed by a reduction once they were passed. In the later seventeenth century, at any rate, rates rose by a sort of ratchet mechanism, in steps from crisis to crisis [Slack, 1988, *175–8*]. Reductions were more common in the early eighteenth century, as in Norwich in the 1730s; but it is not unlikely that there was still some slack in the system left by a fall in casual payments in the second quarter of the eighteenth century. If so, it could easily be taken up, not only by expenditure on the workhouses discussed in the next chapter, but by more and larger pensions to the impotent and especially the old. When between 9 and 10 per cent of the population were over 60, as they were from 1656 to 1726, there could be no lack of pressure on the demand side to mop up any surplus funds. The impotent alone might indeed have consumed all that was available in 1750. In general terms it is arguable that the rise in expenditure between 1696 and 1750 was caused by rising expectations, particularly with respect to the elderly, which the country could afford to meet.

In the second half of the eighteenth century, the situation was different. Prices and population were rising again, and although the proportion of the old declined slightly, the proportion of children in the population grew and with it what is called the 'dependency ratio' – the number of people who had to be supported by those able to work [Wrigley and Schofield, 1981, *443–4, 528–9*]. The consequences can be seen in an increase in the number of casual or extraordinary payments to the able-bodied and in supplementary expenditure generally directed towards labourers and their families [Hampson, 1934, *182, 189*; Hastings, 1982, *11*; Hinton, 1940–2, *174*]. Along with economic pressure came changing perceptions and expectations. In the seventeenth century relief expenditure per head of population seems to have been greatest in towns and industrial areas; by the later eighteenth century it was particularly high in solidly agricultural areas.[8] The impact of enclosure may have had something to do with the change, at least in the Midland counties; but it also required a new awareness of rural indigence on the part of justices and the managers of the machine. Rural poverty was 'discovered' through the debates and discussions about poor relief in county sessions after 1750, in much the same way that the labouring poor were revealed by the urban census-takers of the later sixteenth and early seventeenth centuries.

Whatever the reasons for it, however, the rise in expenditure on the poor between the 1690s and 1780s was real. As column 5 of Table 1 shows, the proportion of the national income being redistributed by these means probably doubled to 2 per cent by 1785. It is impossible to say how large a proportion of the population benefited: many more than the 11 per cent suggested in column 4 for that date, as has already been indicated. By the 1690s regular pensioners were already 5 or 6 per cent of the population of some towns; and casual recipients would probably double their number [Slack, 1988, *174–8*]. In the poorer parts of later Stuart towns a quarter of the population might be either permanently or temporarily on relief. Local variations of this kind make averages meaningless. The limited information so far available for the eighteenth century suggests that pensioners commonly ranged from 1 to 10 per cent of the population of a parish, and we have to add those getting casual relief [Thirsk, 1967/85, V.i. *313*; Arkell, 1987, *40, 42*; Brown, 1984, *410*; Ripley, 1985, *197*]. Surveys of the numbers receiving relief of any kind in a parish over a five-year period in the later eighteenth century might well reveal proportions of 20 per cent or more.

Rate-payers were still more numerous, of course: between a third and two-thirds of householders in different places. In some towns a half of all householders were already being rated by 1700, and that suggests that effective ceilings were reached quite early [Slack, 1988, *177–82*; Brown, 1984, *410*; Ashby, 1912, *29*]. If so, unless populations grew, rising expenditure could only be met by increasing the pound rate, and hence the burden on individual rate-payers – not all of whom could benefit (and many of whom might suffer) from rising wheat prices [Snell, 1985, *90–1*]. The per capita figures in column 2 of Table 1 may therefore tell us more than the deflated figures in column 3 about rate-payers' perceptions. What they saw was the rise between 1750 and 1783, and no doubt in reality between 1760 and 1783. The mounting burden must have been especially noticeable when poor rates rose more quickly than other taxes. The expenditure figures in Table 1 were equal to about 11 per cent of the central government's revenues from direct and excise taxes in 1700 and 12 per cent in 1750, but about 19 per cent in the 1770s and 1780s (and 21 per cent in 1800).[9]

Rising costs can be measured and explained in different ways, but they had to be paid for like any other other item of government expenditure. It is scarcely surprising that, from the later seventeenth century onwards, there were attempts to reform the law in order to keep costs down.

3 *The Failure of Reform*

'Amost every proposal which hath been made for the reformation
of the poor laws hath been tried in former ages and found ineffec-
tual', wrote Richard Burn in 1764.[10] In the 1690s and first decade
of the eighteenth century, in 1723 and 1735, in the early 1750s and
from the 1760s to the 1780s, there was repeated parliamentary
discussion of reform; modifications were made to local practice;
but the structure was not remodelled and costs were not cut. In
the course of debate, in Parliament and the press, three areas of
concern were highlighted. First was the problem of defining the
limits to entitlement to relief: who might legitimately receive poor
relief in the parish? Secondly, given that the entitled universe
was still large, and that its knowledge of its entitlements was
growing, there was the problem of restricting relief only to the
truly deserving: could the undeserving be deterred from claiming
assistance and made self-supporting by the provision of work or
other means? Thirdly, there was the problem of the generous or
inefficient overseer: how should he be supervised and how could
he be prevented from taking the easy course of providing casual
doles or regular pensions to all who applied? The three problems
overlapped in the continuing debate. It will perhaps aid clarity,
however, if we separate them in what follows.

(i) ENTITLEMENT AND SETTLEMENT

It was generally accepted in the later seventeenth and eighteenth centuries that the poor had a right to relief in cases of
extreme necessity, or 'indigency', as it came to be termed. It
was even more generally agreed that this right had become a
legal entitlement under the Elizabethan statutes. Some radical

35

critics wished to abolish the legal obligation to give relief, and return the duty to the realm of private charity [Slack, 1988, *192*; Himmelfarb, 1984, *75–6*]. But most commentators did not go so far. For them the question was how to regulate and police the entitlements which existed.

The concept of 'settlement' provided an early and partial solution. The notion that everyone had a parish of settlement, to which he or she could be returned if they wandered, was implicit in much local and national legislation of the sixteenth and seventeenth centuries, in the vagrancy laws, for example. But it was formalised and made uniform in the law of settlement, beginning with the Act of Settlement of 1662 and amended by later enactments. The original statute of 1662 was essentially an Act for Removal. Newcomers thought 'likely to be chargeable' to a parish could be removed by two justices of the peace, provided that complaint was made against them within 40 days of arrival, and provided that they had not rented a house worth £10 a year or more. This was a clear attempt to limit a parish's responsibilities, and as the statute said, it was provoked by the 'continual increase' of the poor which had become 'exceeding burthensome'. It was only as an afterthought that a clause was added permitting continued residence in certain circumstances if newcomers brought a certificate acknowledging responsibility for them from their own parish.

The cards were stacked still more heavily against poor migrants by a statute of 1686 which said that the period of 40 days within which they could be removed was to begin only when they gave notice of their arrival in a parish: if there were no notice, they could be expelled at any time. In the 1690s, however, the law was amended in favour of the migrant. From 1692 a settlement could be earned in a parish, not just by renting property worth £10 a year, but by paying local rates or – more important for the poor – by being bound as an apprentice or hired as a servant and working for a year. Furthermore, an Act of 1697 declared that those with certificates from their home parish could be removed only when they became chargeable and not until then: the 'certificate man' was given a certain security in his new residence, though still denied entitlement to relief there [Styles, 1978; Taylor, 1976; S. and B. Webb, 1927, *314–43*].

The effects of the law of settlement have been much disputed, both by contemporaries and by later historians, and there is as yet no consensus on whether it did more harm than good. The charges against it are essentially two [S. and B. Webb, 1927, *326–33*]. First, it is argued that it created an expensive bureaucratic maze, an unnecessary burden alike on justices of the peace, parish officers and the poor. Secondly, it is said that this heavyweight bureaucracy was a harmful brake on mobility, hampering the movement of population from areas where labour was in surplus to areas where it was required.

One only needs to look at any collection of parish or county records to appreciate the force of the first charge. Parishes had to keep bundles of settlement certificates and approach justices for removal orders; sessions had to hear appeal after appeal against removal and deal with disputes between parishes. The absurdity of removing a migrant from one parish to another in the same town, and of settlement squabbles between small, often neighbouring parishes in the countryside, was one powerful argument for larger poor-law units, the unions and incorporations which will be discussed later. Although no one has yet computed what proportion of the population was dealt with in one way or another by the law of settlement, they must be reckoned in their tens of thousands; and the surviving records are certainly numerous enough to be a useful source for the history of the eighteenth century labouring poor [Snell, 1985].

It is doubtful, however, whether the law encompassed enough people to be an effective brake on economically useful migration – the second charge. This was still a mobile society, and although there was less *long-distance* mobility in the later seventeenth and early eighteenth centuries than there had been in the later sixteenth and early seventeenth, there were other reasons besides the settlement law for that [Clark and Souden, 1987, *213–52*]. In some respects the law positively sanctioned, even encouraged, migration – for apprentices and for servants for a year. It is true that it was not until 1795 that all migrants gained the security of the 'certificate man', in that they could not be removed until they became chargeable. Until then parish authorities were able to use the law as a flexible weapon. But they used it selectively – to prevent the residence of those who were, or might easily become, a burden. Those removed under the settlement laws were overwhelmingly women and men with families – not young male employable labourers. The latter were allowed to remain. It was not in anyone's interest to prevent their movement to parishes where labour was needed and it continued on a large scale [Hampson, 1934, *138–40*; Clark and Souden, 1987, *279*; Landau, 1988].

The poor migrant – whether young or old, male or female – found it more difficult to earn a new settlement (and hence entitlement to relief), however, than to move to a new residence; and that was the main purpose of the law. In many eighteenth century parishes as much as a fifth of the population might be 'unsettled', and labourers in husbandry were sometimes hired for less than a year in order to keep them so. Consequently, although there are cases of unsettled paupers being given doles, the chief effect of the settlement laws must have been to deter the migrant poor from claiming relief – for fear that they might then be moved out. The law thus limited the burden on local rates and that was its advantage from the point of view of parish officers.

Yet it also had advantages from the point of view of the poor: provided they had an acknowledged settlement, they had an entitlement to relief. They might not find their settlement easy to prove, especially if they were women or children needing to show a 'derivative' settlement from husband or parents. But the law recognised that they had a settlement somewhere and their parish, once identified, could be compelled to support them. From time to time overseers even paid relief to their 'out-poor', resident in other parishes. A modern study of the workings of the law concludes that it acted as a useful cushion, allowing parishes to control mobility but not preventing it, giving the poor local attachments but allowing them some opportunity to establish themselves elsewhere [Taylor, 1976. Cf. Landau, 1988; Snell, 1985, *72, 107*].

If the settlement laws were used selectively to regulate entitlement and mobility, so too were the older vagrancy laws. They were modified in the eighteenth century, however, and employed rather differently. Under new vagrancy statutes in 1714, 1740 and 1744, the summary whippings inflicted by constables according to the 1598 Act were gradually replaced by simple passes or periods of hard labour in houses of correction, at the discretion of justices of the peace. From 1700 also the cost of transporting vagrants was to be met, not by the expelling parish, but from a county rate. Expelling someone as a vagrant then became a cheap and straightforward way of removing them, and this may help to explain an otherwise puzzling change in the character of those caught in the vagrancy net. In the eighteenth century the majority of them were no longer the young adults, largely male, of the later sixteenth and early seventeenth centuries; rather, like some of those removed under the settlement laws, they were predominantly women and the old [Cockburn, 1963–6, *509, 512*. Cf. Clark and Souden, 1987, *56–7*; Beier, 1985, *52*]. Magisterial discretion could use the vagrancy laws to police the boundaries of the welfare system.

This is not to say that the vagrancy laws did not still have a more literal and rudimentary police function: the periods of hard labour and elaborate descriptions of the 'idle and disorderly' in the statutes of 1740 and 1744 testify to that. There was a temporary panic about the disorders of the poor in the early 1740s, thanks to dearth and war, and a more serious one in the 1780s, fanned by a movement for the Reformation of Manners, after the Gordon Riots and with war again. Between the 1690s and the 1780s, however, the wandering loitering able-bodied poor do not seem to have posed the threat they had presented in the later sixteenth and early seventeenth centuries. Rather, the settled poor, those to whom the settlement laws had given a new security, now posed the greater problem: how could they be prevented from being charges on the parish?

(ii) DETERRENCE AND WORK

Deterring the poor from claiming pensions and doles would scarcely have been necessary if the work for the able-bodied promised in the Elizabethan statutes had been realised. It was not. Some parishes still had stocks of materials on which to set the poor to work in the eighteenth century, but they were few in number [S. and B. Webb, 1927, *162*; Hampson, 1934, *187*; Edmonds, 1966, *20*]. Pauper apprentices were much more common, especially after 1697 when fines could be imposed on employers who refused to take them on: they could be numbered in their hundreds in some eighteenth century towns [Hampson, 1934, *152–5*; Anderson, 1981, *112*; Hinton, 1940–2, *183*]. Unemployed or underemployed adults were a more intractable problem, however. Sometimes they were set to work on roads. Sometimes, especially in the later eighteenth century, arrangements could be made for local masters to employ them in turn, by a 'roundsman' system. In areas of surplus labour, however, market forces dictated low wages which had to be made up by 'allowances' at the parish expense. Allowances supplementing wages became a major burden after the end of our period; but they had begun before the 1780s and they were a symptom of the failure of the system to create employment and thus curb outdoor relief [Marshall, 1926, *104–7*; Ashby, 1912, *155*].

The cry therefore went up for some mechanism of deterrence whenever rising rates forced themselves on contemporary attention. The 1697 statute attempted to reinforce shame sanctions – the stigma of being on the parish – by insisting that poor pensioners should wear badges indicating their status. Whether through the negligence or the sensitivity of overseers, the practice never became general [S. and B. Webb, 1927, *160–1*]. The only clear alternative was to make the conditions of relief themselves unattractive; and the obvious way of doing that – in the eighteenth century as in the nineteenth – was by moving paupers to special institutions and denying outdoor relief to anyone who refused to enter. This was the option sanctioned, but not insisted upon, in the Workhouse Test Act of 1723, also known as Knatchbull's Act.

Before we look at the effects of that Act, and the success or otherwise of deterrence, however, it is important to stress that workhouses were never wholly or even mainly visualised as deterrent institutions. They had much more positive functions. We have seen that the moral reform of the poor was central from the beginning, from Bridewell onwards. Recognition of the economic utility of labour-discipline was also an established theme, chiming in with projects for new trades in the first half of the seventeenth century, and with envy of the Dutch, whose workhouses were often held out as a model, in the second half. Morality and economy in fact went hand in hand in the attacks

on the idleness and leisure preferences of the poor which pro-
liferated after 1660. In the writings of Thomas Firmin, John
Bellers, John Cary and the other advocates of workhouses, their
beneficial effect on the probity and character of the poor was at
least as important as their economic return to the nation and to
the rate-payer [Appleby, 1978, *136–42*; Hitchcock, 1987, *viii–xiv*].

Motives shifted slightly over time and from pressure group
to pressure group. The national economy and the rate burden
were no doubt foremost in the minds of members of the Board of
Trade in 1695 and 1696, who discussed various projects for pauper
institutions, including John Locke's proposal for 'working schools'
in every parish. On the other hand, 'Societies for the Reformation
of Manners' – local associations intent on suppressing popular
vices such as swearing and drunkenness – were often important
in the background to the new 'Corporations of the Poor', which
established large workhouses in fourteen towns, from Bristol to
Norwich, between 1696 and 1712. Their model was the London
Corporation of the Interregnum, which was also revived, and
John Cary, instigator of the Bristol Corporation, hoped that
their example might in turn be copied in counties as well as
towns [Slack, 1988, *195–200*; Innes, 1987, *79*; Macfarlane, 1986].
Sir Humphrey Mackworth similarly wanted 'factories' in every
parish, and introduced bills into Parliament for that purpose
between 1704 and 1707. The bills failed, partly because Daniel
Defoe attacked their economic rationale: such work-schemes
would create no new trades but would take away work from
those already employed [Ransome, 1948].

Yet the quest for moral reform continued. By the second
and third decades of the eighteenth century the Society for the
Promotion of Christian Knowledge (SPCK) was as interested in
promoting workhouses as charity schools, and for similar reasons;
and parishes faced with rising rates after the Spanish Succession
War began to respond. They founded their own workhouses, or
contracted to have their poor housed and managed by private
entrepreneurs, men like Matthew Marryott, who ran more than
a score of houses, the first at Olney, Buckinghamshire, in 1714.
The 1723 Act thus gave recognition and stimulus to a workhouse
movement which had already begun.[11] It popularised the workhouse test, encouraged contracting for the relief of the poor, and

permitted unions of parishes for workhouse purposes [Hampson, 1934, *72–83*; Oxley, 1969]. An *Account of Several Workhouses*, published under the auspices of the SPCK in 1725, could list 129 such institutions. By 1732 there were probably more than 700 of them, and a second *Account* applauded their success in towns such as Reading where lavish outdoor relief was curbed as effectively as 'idleness and sloth'.

It is questionable, however, whether deterrence worked in anything more than the shortest of short terms. At Stroud in 1729 rates were said to have been cut by half since the workhouse was founded in 1722.[12] They also fell in Liverpool after a house was opened in 1733 [Blease, 1909, *112*]. But continuing success depended on eternal vigilance and a stern refusal to grant outdoor relief, and these were difficult to maintain in the face of prevailing conceptions of charity and changing economic circumstances. Even if achieved, success meant that workhouses became houses of refuge for the old and impotent poor, whose claims could not be denied or deterred, not the houses of profitable productive industry, paying their way, that projectors had hoped for. More often, outdoor relief for both impotent and able-bodied slowly returned, not only and inevitably in large towns such as Hull, Liverpool and Leeds, but in smaller places like Eaton Socon, Bedfordshire, where by 1730 rates were back where they had been before a workhouse was opened in 1719 [Jackson, 1972, *322*; Blease, 1909, *121*; Anderson, 1981, *88*; Oxley, 1969, *36*; Emmison, 1933, *4, 27*].

In many parishes the costs of poor relief were certainly relatively stable between the 1720s and the 1750s, except for occasional bad years, like the winter of 1740–1; but these included parishes like Tysoe, Warwickshire, which did not have workhouses, as well as those that did [Ashby, 1912, *184*; Edmonds, 1966]. It is difficult to avoid the conclusion that in general it was good times – low prices and reasonably full employment, rather than good management or the workhouse test – which kept expenditure down. That, however, gave workhouses a spurious reputation for real achievement. It is not surprising that they were the acknowledged panacea when another spurt of reforming activity gathered momentum after 1750, fuelled by fears of national decadence and declining population in time of war, and reflected in a spate of pamphlets and Local Acts of Parliament 'improving' poor relief along with other local services and amenities. There were roughly one hundred of these statutes between 1748 and 1783 [Oxley, 1974, *22–3*; Eden, 1797, III, *cclvii ff.*].

The most notable practical results were to be seen in East Anglia, where groups of parishes were incorporated, 'houses of industry' founded, and outdoor relief cut back. The first incorporation was at Nacton in Suffolk in 1756, sponsored by the national hero, Admiral Vernon, and a group of concerned gentlemen; and there were thirteen others in Norfolk and Suffolk by 1785 [S. and B. Webb, 1927, *126–36*; Digby, 1978, *1, 32–4*]. New houses also sprang up elsewhere. By 1782 it is likely that at least a third of all parishes, and probably more, either had their own or had access to one through incorporation or contract. These parishes also continued with outdoor relief, however, and their workhouses could not achieve even partial success, once population, prices and unemployment, especially rural unemployment, started rising again after 1760. Pensions and casual payments everywhere increased [S. and B. Webb, 1927, *138–42*; Brown, 1984, *182–9*; Blease, 1909, *122*; Fearn, 1958, *109*; Hastings, 1982, *7*; Hinton, 1940–2, *194–5*]; and public anxiety about the consequences for the rates mounted again.

Its course is well reflected in the career of Thomas Gilbert, who published a succession of proposals, and introduced a series of parliamentary bills, for national reform of the law. Gilbert's *Scheme* of 1764 rested firmly on houses of industry and allowed only occasional and temporary outdoor relief. By 1781, however, partly prompted by Richard Burn's argument that outdoor relief was cheaper than institutional support, he was plainly having second thoughts; and this time his *Plan* led to successful legislation.[13] Gilbert's Act of 1782, the first general reform since the Workhouse Test Act, faced facts. It left several options open to local authorities, but if they adopted the Act, they should only house the impotent in workhouses. The able-bodied poor were to be found employment outside, and supported from the rates if wages were inadequate or employment could not be found. Both prescriptions were already established practice in many localities.

Gilbert's Act has often been regarded as a vital turning point, from institutional to outdoor relief. Like the 1723 statute, however, it reflected rather than initiated local realities. It reflected also a gradual swing of opinion against workhouses in general. Popular opinion probably counted for little, since it was always adverse. Plans for an incorporated workhouse in East Anglia in 1765 met with riots: people wanted relief in their 'own' parishes and would 'fight for their liberties' [Snell, 1985, 73]. More influential were revelations of mismanagement and cruelty in some houses, and the growing suspicion that most of them in practice inculcated the idleness and vice they were supposed to repress. Although the Webbs took such complaints too much at face value, and many workhouses were in fact efficiently and humanely run, there is no doubt about the strength of the reaction against them [S. and B. Webb, 1927, 141–4, 233–45; Digby, 1978, 37–46].

It probably owed something to a remarkable burst of philanthropic activity in mid century, prodded by men such as Jonas Hanway, who publicised the misery and mortality of workhouse children in London [Taylor, 1985]. It has also been argued that a more 'generous way of thinking' and more sympathetic attitude towards the poor became generally prevalent from the 1750s [Coats, 1960, 48–9; Coats, 1976, 108; Marshall, 1926, 55–6]. Like the stress on 1782 as a turning point, however, that is too tidy – and arguably romantic – a view. It attributes too much influence in the early eighteenth century to attacks on charity like Bernard Mandeville's *Fable of the Bees* (1723) (which was as likely to provoke as to dull tender consciences); and it ignores the idealism which the SPCK brought to the early workhouse movement and the quest for another Reformation of Manners which accompanied the rethinking of the 1780s. Benevolence, moral reform and economy marched together throughout the eighteenth century.

The real reason for the changing perception of institutions after 1750 was not greater benevolence but a more realistic scepticism about what they could achieve. The 1732 *Account of Workhouses* hoped to kill several birds with its one stone: workhouses would 'answer all the ends of charity to the poor, in regard to their souls and bodies; and yet at the same time prove effectual expedients for increasing our manufactures, as well as removing a heavy burden from the nation'.[14] The aspirations were the same in the 1760s and 1770s, but few were convinced that houses of industry or refuge alone could deliver all the goods. There remained one further possibility: greater control over parish overseers of the poor.

(iii) GUARDIANS AND OVERSEERS

The inadequacies of the parochial basis of the poor law had been evident from the beginning. The levying of 'rates in aid' from rich parishes, undertaken by justices of the peace, particularly in towns, under the provisions of Elizabethan statutes, was a recognition that poverty and the wealth needed to relieve it might be unequally distributed. Parishes were also usually too small to engage in expensive projects for poor relief. The attempted centralisation of welfare in Tudor London through the hospitals was one attempt to get round that, although the 1598 Act effectively brought it to an end. Many of the later efforts to create workhouses rested on combinations of parishes: the London Corporation of the Poor of 1647; the Corporations of the 1690s; the unions of parishes – fragile though they were – permitted under the Workhouse Test Act of 1723; and the incorporated unions, like those in East Anglia, set up under local Acts of Parliament from the 1750s onwards.

It was not, however, simply a matter of larger units providing greater resources. At the root of all these schemes was a distrust of the overseers. Complaints about their 'partiality', 'misconduct' and 'laxity' mounted from the 1660s right up to the Poor Law Amendment Act of 1834. Their readiness to grant doles and casual payments to any who came was generally regarded as the reason for rising costs. A statute of 1692 sought to control 'the unlimited power' of overseers and churchwardens, 'who do frequently, upon frivolous pretences (but chiefly for their own private ends) give relief to what persons and number they think fit'. Vestries were to examine lists of pensioners every Easter and to approve only those they thought 'fit to receive collection'; and no additions should be permitted except by authority of a justice of the peace. The Act had no effect. Neither did further statutes in 1723 and 1744, making overseers declare the needs of paupers on oath before justices could order relief and prescribing public notice of rates before they were levied. In reality, vestries felt the same responsibilities under the Elizabethan statutes as overseers; and so did justices of the peace, who ordered additional relief to individual paupers more often than they refused it. As the 1832 Poor Law Commissioners noted, the latter were on the one hand 'empowered to enforce charity and liberality by summons and fine' and on the other deterred by other business and a lack of detailed knowledge from exercising the close supervision which was required [S. G. and E. O. A. Checkland, 1974, *181–2, 221, 241*].

There was hence a continuing search for a new kind of poor-law authority whose sole concern should be the oversight of social welfare. The London Corporation of the Poor of the Interregnum, with its 52 governing Assistants, 10 of them aldermen and the rest freemen elected from the wards of the city, was one attempt. The new corporations set up by local statutes from 1696 to 1712 repeated the story. The first, that in Bristol, was governed by the mayor and aldermen and 48 'Guardians' elected by the ratepayers in the parishes. Though not all of them had directly elected governors, other urban Corporations of the Poor similarly brought together existing office-holders and men outside the magistracy (often Dissenters, even Quakers) in a new corporate body with a particular purpose. Moreover, all sought to control parish overseers, generally in two ways: first by imposing a ceiling on the rates at their existing level, and secondly by administering as much relief as possible through a central workhouse with paid officials. All these elements were to be copied, in one way or another, in later attempts at reform.

Equally continuous, however, were the political problems which beset the corporations. Parishes resisted efforts to control their charities, rates and disbursements and they were often successful. In Bristol, for example, the corporation effectively surrendered to parochial pressure when all churchwardens were made *ex officio* Guardians in 1714. At the same time, town councils were suspicious of these rival authorities and reluctant to see them become too independent. That conflict sometimes took the form of Tory magistrates opposing Whig corporations [Slack, 1988, *196–200*; Wright, 1988, *169*]. But its roots lay deeper than mere party politics. Magistrates were bound to have, if not second thoughts, then mixed feelings about divesting themselves of troublesome responsibilities if that meant a palpable dilution of their status and authority under the law. Given these difficulties, it is easy to see why all later modifications to the administrative structure of the system were either voluntary or local. They depended on consent.

The Workhouse Test Act of 1723 allowed parishes to try to keep costs down by combining and/or contracting for the relief of the poor. It could be effective if parish officers cooperated. In south Lancashire they paid governors to run union workhouses. Elsewhere they might use workhouses managed by voluntary boards. In the large parish of Leeds, the vestry had a committee of Guardians who took over the whole administration of poor relief [Oxley, 1969; Anderson, 1981, 79–80]. Magistrates could be similarly energetic on a local basis. A bill of 1735, based on William Hay's scheme for unions of parishes controlled by Guardians who should be gentlemen of 'estate', failed. But the Acts establishing incorporated unions in East Anglia from the 1750s were essentially local versions of the same thing. Justices of the peace joined with men of property in a board of Guardians of the Poor, and they in turn appointed 'Acting Guardians' to manage a workhouse, employ officials, and determine what outdoor relief should be given by the overseers [S. and B. Webb, 1927, 129–32, 265–6].

There was naturally some parochial resistance, as there had been to the earlier municipal corporations; but that did nothing to dampen parliamentary enthusiasm for such unions, provided that they were supported by local propertied interests, and provided that they did not threaten the position of the magistracy too obviously. Thomas Gilbert's *Scheme* of 1764 owed a good deal to the East Anglian incorporations: it placed overseers under the control of Guardians who should include, besides justices of the peace, parish priests and freeholders of land worth more than £30. Yet it failed to appeal as a national remedy to Parliament in 1765. What did appeal was Gilbert's Act of 1782 which, while still recommending unions in which overseers should be reduced to mere collectors of rates, left localities free to choose, and (if they chose reform) placed the appointment of Guardians in the hands of justices of the peace [S. and B. Webb, 1927, 272–5].

Gilbert himself saw his Act as inadequate. It was a 'temporary expedient' until more extensive plans could be agreed, and he had more radical solutions in mind. In another abortive *Bill* of 1786 he proposed statutory commissions to divide every county into districts, and district committees with salaried agents managing the relief of the poor. Here were some familiar themes: paid officials and larger units curbing the independence of overseers. But here too was a recognition of the need for a new structure of local government to make reform work. As Gilbert's *Plan of Police*, also published in 1786, acknowledged, one objection to it was its threat to the position of justices of the peace.[15]

Parliament was unwilling to grasp that particular nettle in the eighteenth century. It approved permissive legislation. It favoured local Acts, sometimes of a relatively radical kind, promoted by local lobbies committed to and involved in reform. Individual MPs like Gilbert engaged in long debate over strategies, consulted magistrates, took surveys of the costs and mechanisms of relief [Innes, 1990; Poynter, 1969, *13*]. But they were not ready to countenance a radical reform of the whole of local government from the centre. It needed another generation of rising rates to bring a Parliament of landowners and magistrates to the point of change; and even in the 1830s it is debatable how much they welcomed it [Mandler, 1987]. Yet Gilbert's publications show that the writing was on the wall by the 1780s, and what it spelled out was that the welfare machine was so integral a part of the structure of local government that the refom of the first could only be achieved by reform of the second.

4 *The Law in Context*

The formal mechanisms of statutory relief described above were, of course, only one of the ways in which help could be given to the poor. There were also various kinds of philanthropy, from alms distributed casually in the streets to formally established charitable institutions. The fact that people's benevolence extended far beyond the rates paid for the poor affected their view of what the poor law should accomplish. It also added considerably to the aggregate resources transferred from rich to poor, and so complicates any attempt to measure what the law did in fact achieve. Finally, it raises once again the question of why the poor law was necessary at all, since philanthropy proved adequate in other countries. Setting the poor law in its context entails asking what it was about English attitudes or the English system of government which made its social-welfare system unique.

(i) BENEVOLENCE

Charity was undeniably one of the impulses behind the poor law: the law was necessary, Tudor Englishmen felt, because some forms of charitable activity were in decline. But the poor law also set out to reform and remodel charity. It should be purposive and discriminatory. Begging and casual almsgiving were to be abolished. The generous instincts of donors should be disciplined by attention to the recipients. 'Beneficence' – *doing* good – was a commonly praised virtue in the later sixteenth century. The important subject of developing concepts and practices of charity has yet to be given the historical attention it deserves, but it is clear that both the purposes and mechanisms of philanthropy altered substantially between 1530 and 1780.

W. K. Jordan's volumes on the charitable giving recorded in wills between 1480 and 1660 have probably exaggerated the degree and pace of change [Jordan, 1959; 1960]. He shows without any question that large and increasing sums of money were being given by testators for the relief of the poor between 1540 and 1660, particularly to found almshouses and establish charitable doles. Even when we take into account inflation, the yield from these endowments was rising and, moreover, keeping pace with population growth [Bittle and Lane, 1976; Hadwin, 1978]. However, by concentrating on major benefactors, most of them London merchants, and on formal endowments, Jordan underestimated the importance of the small sums left by hundreds of smaller donors, usually in the form of once-for-all cash hand-outs to the poor. Funeral doles of an indiscriminate kind did not significantly decline in popularity until the end of the seventeenth century.

Concentration on wills as evidence for philanthropy also entails the neglect of giving *inter vivos*, gifts made while donors were still alive. We have no means of measuring casual charity, alms given to the poor in the yard of an inn or at a man's door. There is no doubt that it continued to the end of our period: there would not have been beggars in the streets of London and other towns if it had not. It is likely that there was a decline in what we might call neighbourly charity: it was one purpose of the poor law to stop the poor of a parish begging from door to door. But if the beggar was more often a stranger than a known neighbour by 1700, it is clear from contemporary descriptions that he had not disappeared.

In the later seventeenth and eighteenth centuries, however, a new form of *inter vivos* charity developed, of major importance for our theme. That was 'associated philanthropy': the funding of charitable activity by subscriptions from a large number of benefactors [Owen, 1964, *11–12, 71–2*]. Based partly on the example of joint-stock companies, partly on the ways in which sects such as the Quakers financed themselves, charitable subscriptions gradually usurped the place once occupied by the charitable endowment by will. Charity schools, which could be numbered in their hundreds by 1750, were the greatest manifestation of this new philanthropy in the early eighteenth century, and hospitals later. Five Voluntary Hospitals had been founded in London by 1760, the first of them the Westminster in 1720, and there were 21 in the provinces by 1775 [Thomas, 1980, *3–4*; Woodward, 1974, *36*]. Public concern for the physical and moral health of the nation in mid century was also reflected in charities directed towards children and women, which attracted enormous sums in subscriptions and gifts, from Thomas Coram's Foundling Hospital of 1739, through Jonas Hanway's Marine Society, to the Magdalen Hospital for 'poor, young, thoughtless females' of 1758. These objects appealed, as Joseph Massie said, to the several motives of 'Charity, Humanity, Patriotism and Economy' [McClure, 1981; Nash, 1984; Taylor, 1985, *182*].

It was a characteristically Georgian mixture. Yet there are also elements in this broadly based 'associated philanthropy' which remind us of the sixteenth century. Its targets and its non-parochial organisation were not unlike those of the mid-Tudor hospitals of London. The close, if not quite face-to-face, involvement of Georgian benefactors in charitable activity, and their attempts to reform those such as prostitutes who were beyond the respectable pale, are even reminiscent of the 'new' Catholic philanthropy and fraternities of Counter-Reformation Europe [cf. Pullan, 1988, *194–5*]. There was furthermore a pious charge in much early eighteenth century philanthropy, with men such as Robert Nelson stressing redemption and the intentions of donors as well as recipients in ways which seem closer to the mid sixteenth century than to the mid seventeenth. It may or may not be significant that Georgian Englishmen took pride in 'benevolence' not 'beneficence': the attitudes of benefactors perhaps mattered as much as their acts [Himmelfarb, 1984, *36*].

There was something of the character of fraternities also in the hundreds of 'friendly societies' which sprang up in England in the century after 1660, and which provided, among other things, mutual protection for their members against illness and misfortune [Clark, 1988]. Here again were associations of a kind little known between 1550 and 1650, though trade gilds and companies had some of their functions. As with subscription charities, it may be that they flourished in the early eighteenth

51

century because the country could then afford them. But they too show that the poor law did not satisfy all the needs, either of the poor or of the benevolent. The poor still preferred self-help to the stigma of the dole, despite increasing notions of entitlement. Benefactors in their thousands wanted more active involvement than simply paying rates.

The result, by 1780, must have been the transfer of very large sums indeed to the poor on top of the rates, though it is impossible to quantify them. Jordan's figures suggest that in 1660 the total income from his charities was about £100,000 per annum, roughly the same, perhaps, as the income from poor rates at that date [Slack, 1988, *171*]. The number of charitable trusts probably doubled in the following century, and a parliamentary inquiry estimated their income in 1788 at £258,700. The 1788 returns had many omissions, however, and they take no account at all of the various forms of associated philanthropy [Owen, 1964, *72–4*; Wilson, 1981]. We certainly cannot conclude that formal charity was in 1788 contributing only 10 per cent of the amount raised by the rates. It is possible that, just as in 1660, it was providing quite as much as public assistance. In towns, which not only had hospitals but also subscriptions in response to temporary crises (1763 in Leeds, 1784 in Manchester), private charity may even have been the major partner: a situation the reverse of that suggested by local studies of the mid seventeenth century [Anderson, 1981, *96*; Hindle, 1975, *107–8*; cf. Christie, 1984, *122*; Slack, 1988, *170*].

Whatever their size, charitable investments of this kind were bound to give ammunition to those like Joseph Townsend in the later eighteenth century who argued that massive poor rates were unnecessary. Self-help, friendly societies and purposeful charitable subscriptions should be enough. Yet what Townsend admired as 'the mild complacency of benevolence' was also, in less complacent form, the public attitude which informed the practice of the poor law, limiting its harshness and extending its boundaries.[16] The language of charity and the language of entitlements and obligations under the law were different, and could sometimes be in tension with one another [cf. Mandler, 1987]; but the second would have been inconceivable without the first.

(ii) POVERTY

If payments to the poor were in aggregate as large as has been suggested, what was their impact on poverty? It cannot have been very great in the century before 1660. Poor rates were too small and the number of the poor too large. Outdoor relief, charitable doles and such government activities as the regulation of the grain trade must have done something to save some people from destitution and starvation – especially in the poorer parts of towns and the richer parts of southern England, which already had rates; but they did not prevent malnutrition in bad years in the North or that general impoverishment of the labouring poor suggested by our sources for the half-century after 1580.

In the century after 1660, of course, things changed. Poor rates rose to 1 per cent or so of national income, enabling 8 per cent of the population to be relieved by 1750; and philanthropy would add substantially to those figures. It was not this, however, which improved the condition of the poor in early Hanoverian England, important though it was in individual crisis years and for disadvantaged groups such as the old. The important factor was general economic change which raised living standards overall. The crucial question in this period is not whether poor relief conquered poverty, for it did not, but whether it retarded or accelerated economic growth.

Some eighteenth century critics took a negative view, arguing that poor relief destroyed incentives to work, and did nothing to increase productivity. It seems probable, however, that this is too pessimistic. The sort of production undertaken in workhouses probably had little effect either way, given its size, though it is possible to argue against Defoe that make-work schemes did spread new trades in the seventeenth century, though not perhaps in the eighteenth when they were no longer so novel [Thirsk, 1978, 65–6]. More important, transfers of wealth from rich to poor of the sort we have considered must have had some modest impact on consumer demand, and that should not be neglected, given that the transfers were, in part at least, 'to persons with a high propensity to consume from those with a comparatively high propensity to save' [Coats, 1976, 113].

After 1760, and still more after 1780, the situation changed

53

again. Expenditure from the rates continued to increase, but so too did the number of the labouring poor, as population and prices rose. Welfare payments slowly shifted their incidence from the old and impotent to the able-bodied, who received them either for themselves or in respect of their children. These circumstances produced that attack on public relief from Malthus and other critics which led to the report of the 1832 Royal Commission and the widespread allegation that the system encouraged pauperisation by subsidising early marriage, large families and low wages.

The accuracy of that critique has been much debated. There have been different views about the extent to which relief went to the able-bodied and what effects that might have had [Blaug, 1963; Boyer, 1986; Huzel, 1969; Marshall, 1968/85; Williams, 1981]. Although these debates refer essentially to the half-century after 1782, they indicate two conclusions relevant to the earlier history of the poor law. First, they suggest that the welfare system was confronting a real problem of poverty, particularly in rural England, in the hard times of the 1780s: and the fact that it was capable of meeting, though not entirely overcoming, it was no mean achievement. Secondly (though this is more disputed), they suggest that the machinery of poor relief responded to *demand*; it did not, as its critics would argue, create it.

To see social welfare as largely and in general 'demand-led' rather than 'supply-led' seems reasonable enough. To put it crudely, the welfare system responded to economic and demographic facts, trying to meet the needs of children and the able-bodied 'labouring poor' before 1630, increasingly satisfying the demands of the old from 1660 to 1760, and shifting to the young and able-bodied again after 1780. Yet this picture needs some refinement. We have seen how the welfare machine was to a degree independent of the economic environment, identifying its own particular targets, and how slow it was to change. Its response to changing circumstances was neither voluntary nor immediate. Moreover, given that it was to an extent set in its ways, the levels of expenditure it deployed in the later seventeenth and eighteenth centuries could not be wholly neutral in their impact. It can be argued that heavy expenditure on the poor had a 'positive feed-back effect': that is, that it reinforced certain established features of the social and demographic situation and thus (it may further be argued) to an extent cushioned English society against rapid change.

If this approach is correct, and it should certainly not be pushed too far, then relief payments to labourers with young families at the end of the eighteenth century may have helped to maintain high marriage and fertility rates for a little longer than would otherwise have been the case at a time of declining real wages. To that extent, there may have been something in the Malthusian argument. More important for our purposes, payments to the elderly and to single women in the later seventeenth century may possibly have encouraged the persistence of late marriage and low fertility even when economic conditions were improving.[17] This leads to a more general point, underlined by the work of demographic and family historians. Nuclear families, relatively late ages at marriage and the mobility of adolescent apprentices and servants, all of which characterised England throughout our period, depended on collective support being available for the old. It is significant that the poor law did not in practice hold children responsible for their parents or grandparents (although it made the latter responsible for the former). Hence young people could move, save, marry late and not rush to have offspring of their own who would care for them in sickness or old age. It was vital for much of the fabric of the English economy and society that the elderly in need should be cared for by charity or the state [cf. Smith, 1984; Thomson, 1986].

Another, and perhaps less speculative, positive feedback effect of the poor law lay in the realm of expectations. Eighteenth century poor relief not only did something to maintain living standards in times of distress: levels of nutrition, for example, and hence perhaps economic productivity. It also helped to support rising expectations of what an adequate standard of living was [Coats, 1976, *113–15*]. Some people were kept in styles to which they were becoming accustomed. More important than that, the relief machine ensured that 'poverty' was always being identified, although living standards were rising for much of the century. The poor law owed its origins, at least in part, to public sensitivity to deprivation; and that sensitivity continued, despite the fact that the English poor were never as poor as those of some other European countries and indeed became increasingly less so.

Over the centuries the poor law and its agents thus reinforced that intolerance of relative deprivation which justified their existence.

(iii) POLITICS

The social repercussions of the poor law suggest that it must have had political consequences also. It has often been argued that it helped to preserve political stability, and there is much to be said for the case [Christie, 1984, *116*; Ashby, 1912, *103*]. There were obviously many other factors at work here, and the provision of relief in itself should not be thought of as 'buying off' rebellion or revolution. But the poor law, like abundant charity, must have persuaded people that there was justice in the status quo and to that extent have encouraged deference. It would be possible to go on to argue that the poor law encouraged social and cultural differentiation, increasing the gap between the rough and the respectable, the vulgar and the educated. That, however, has its dangers. We should not think of the poor as passive recipients of doles or charity. They were well able to manipulate the system for their own purposes, entering workhouses, for example, when they needed housing, putting pressure on overseers and if necessary justices when outdoor relief suited them better. Moreover, people moved into and out of poverty, and were rarely for a lifetime subjected to and socialised by the dependent status of the pauper.

In fact, it arguably makes more sense to look at the poor law, not in terms of a 'deference' model, but in terms of a participatory one; and this is certainly the case when we turn our attention to those who enforced and paid for it. We have seen the impact of the law at every level of government, from the executive Council of the early Stuarts, through its agents the assize judges, to magistrates, parish constables and overseers. It was a focus of attention at every point where people participated in public affairs: in the vestry, the town council, quarter sessions and, not least, Parliament. It had its own literature, from Books of Orders, through handbooks for justices, to the pamphlets of commentators and projectors from the 1640s to the 1780s. Because it conferred powers of patronage and financial resources, it created vested interests in parishes and trusts and was often a bone of contention between opposing factions – between Puritans and non-Puritans in early seventeenth century towns or Whigs and Tories fighting to control parishes and Corporations of the Poor in the eighteenth century. Once the system was in operation, radical reform on a national scale was therefore difficult to achieve. But local interest groups could find ways round the stranglehold of parishes and magistrates, including various kinds of incorporation and forms of associated philanthropy; and the system could be reinvigorated from time to time by those reform 'waves' which can be seen in municipalities in the early seventeenth century, both there and among 'Country' members of Parliament in the 1690s, and in the localities and Parliament again in the mid and later eighteenth century. As a result, the poor law was a major factor shaping English political culture.

It was also, of course, a product of it. (Here we have yet another 'chicken-and-egg' or 'positive feed-back' relationship.) If we ask why England alone produced a social-welfare system of this size and complexity, we must find the answer in political habits and structures of government. Scotland provides an instructive point of comparison. Like England, Scotland had a Reformation leaving a vacuum in charitable activity; the social need was even greater; there was even a poor law on paper not unlike England's. But the law had little impact before the end of the seventeenth century. One reason was the 'weakness of the supervisory machinery': a less powerful central executive than south of the border and justices less accustomed to enforcing the law against the vested interests of landowners who resisted rates [Mitchison, 1974]. The English poor law succeeded not just because Parliament could frame practicable strategies, but because Privy Council, assize judges and sessions could enforce them; and it may well be weakness at the county sessions level which explains the failure to implement much of the poor law in Wales until well into the eighteenth century.

It is worth also looking a little further down the chain of government, to the parish. Another reason for the failure of the poor law in Scotland was the absence of anything like the English civil parish; and the same may apply to Wales. One thinks of the civil parish, with some reason, as a product rather than a cause

57

of the poor law. But we need also to ask why vestries and parish elites were able to respond to the demands which the law and the executive made on them in Tudor and early Stuart England; and that turns our attention to the political and welfare activities of townships and parishes before the Reformation [Wright, 1988, *29–84*]. These are topics which are only now being properly investigated, but the poor law may well have rested upon – just as it considerably developed – collective activity, political participation, at the most local level. Not the least of the interests of the poor law is the light it can throw on the nature of English politics, and hence of the English state.

Appendix: Statutes Relating to the Poor

The following summarises the main provisions of the more important statutes. Those with the greatest impact on local practice are marked with an asterisk.

* 1531 *Concerning Punishment of Beggars and Vagabonds* (22 Henry VIII c. 12)

(i) Vagabonds to be whipped (rather than stocked as previously) and returned to place of birth or dwelling for three years.

(ii) Impotent to be licensed to beg by justices, mayor, bailiffs, etc.

1536 *For Punishment of Sturdy Vagabonds and Beggars* (27 Henry VIII c. 25)

(i) Returned vagabonds to be set to work and children put to service.

(ii) Voluntary alms to be collected weekly by churchwardens or two others in every parish for the impotent, and accounted for.

(iii) Casual almsgiving banned, but with many provisos.
(This Act technically lapsed when not renewed later in 1536.)

1547 *For the Punishment of Vagabonds and Relief of the Poor and Impotent Persons* (1 Edw. VI c. 3)

(i) Vagabonds may be bound as slaves for two years.

(ii) Children to be put to service, work provided for aged poor and weekly collections for the impotent, who are not to beg.

1550 *Touching the Punishment of Vagabonds and other Idle Persons* (3 & 4 Edw. VI. c. 16)

(i) 1547 repealed and 1531 restored for vagabonds.

(ii) Poor children to be put to service.

(iii) Impotent to be relieved and not to beg unless licensed.

* 1552 *For the Provision and Relief of the Poor* (5 & 6 Edw. VI c. 2)

(i) 1531 and 1550 confirmed.

(ii) Collectors of alms to be chosen in every parish and to account; inhabitants to agree what they will give weekly.

(iii) Register to be kept of impotent poor on relief, and none to beg.

1555 *For the Relief of the Poor* (2 & 3 Philip & Mary c. 5)

As 1552, but provision for licensed beggars, who are to wear badges.

1563 *For the Relief of the Poor* (5 Eliz, I c. 3)

1555 with additions: those refusing to contribute to the poor after exhortation by a bishop may be bound to appear before JPs who can assess them; fines for those refusing to be collectors for the poor.

* 1572 *For the Punishment of Vagabonds and for Relief of the Poor and Impotent* (14 Eliz. I c. 5)

(i) Earlier statutes repealed.

(ii) Vagabonds to be whipped and burned through the ear by order of sessions, unless taken into service.

(iii) JPs to register names of 'aged, decayed and impotent poor', decide how much they require and assess 'all the inhabitants' to contribute weekly to their relief, on pain of committal to gaol.

(iv) Collectors of assessments and overseers of the poor to be appointed, and monthly 'views and searches' of poor made.

(v) Returned vagabonds to be set to work and children bound to service.

(vi) JPs may license beggars if too many to be relieved otherwise.

1576 *For Setting of the Poor on Work, and for the Avoiding of Idleness* (18 Eliz. I c. 3)

Stocks of materials for poor to work on to be set up in every town, and houses of correction in every county for those refusing to work.

* 1598 *For the Relief of the Poor* (39 Eliz. I c. 30)

(i) Churchwardens and four overseers in every parish to set

children and poor to work, relieve the impotent and bind out pauper children as apprentices, and tax 'every inhabitant and occupier of lands' in the parish for these purposes. They can distrain the goods of those refusing to pay.

(ii) Two JPs to nominate the overseers and take their accounts.

(iii) JPs may tax some parishes to help others and shall (in sessions) hear appeals against rates.

(iv) Begging forbidden except by those allowed to beg food in their own parishes.

* 1598 *For the Punishment of Rogues, Vagabonds and Sturdy Beggars* (39 Eliz. I c. 40)

(i) Earlier Vagrancy Acts repealed.

(ii) Vagabonds to be whipped by order of a JP or of parish officers and sent with passport to place of birth or last dwelling for a year.

(iii) Dangerous and incorrigible rogues to be committed to gaol and may be banished by sessions.

1601 *For the Relief of the Poor* (43 Eliz. I c. 2)

Substantially like the 1598 Relief Act, but reference to begging for food omitted and two overseers sufficient in small parishes.

1604 *For the Charitable Relief and Ordering of Persons infected with the Plague* (1 James I c. 31)

Rates to be levied for the infected and penalties imposed on those leaving infected houses.

1610 *For the Due Execution of . . . Laws . . . Against Rogues . . . and Other Lewd and Idle Persons* (7 James I c. 4)

Houses of correction to be erected in every county for rogues, bastard-bearers and other 'idle and disorderly persons'.

1647 & 1649 (*Ordinances of Parliament for the Relief and Employment of the Poor and the Punishment of Vagrants and other disorderly Persons in the City of London*)

Corporation of the Poor set up in London, with Mayor as President and Assistants partly elected by the wards; to erect workhouses and houses of correction, enforce laws against vagabonds, set poor to work; may ask Common Council for rates for these purposes.

* 1662 *For the better Relief of the Poor of this Kingdom* [Act of Settlement] (13 & 14 Car. II c. 12)

(i) Newcomers to a parish may be removed by 2 JPs if complaint made within 40 days and they have rented houses worth less than £10 p.a. Certificates from the home parish allow residence in some circumstances.

(ii) Continuation of London Corporation of the Poor provided for, and others in Home Counties.

(iii) In large northern parishes, townships to have own overseers etc.

1692 *For . . . supplying the Defects of the former Laws for the Settlement of the Poor* (3 William & Mary c. 11)

(i) Rate-paying, apprenticeship and a year's service earn a settlement.

(ii) Vestries to approve list of pensioners each year and no name to be added except by authority of a JP.

1696 to 1712 Acts (the first for Bristol: 7 & 8 William III c. 32) establishing Corporations of the Poor in 14 towns, with powers to erect workhouses, etc. and varying authority over parishes.

* 1697 *For supplying some Defects in the Laws for the Relief of the Poor* (8 & 9 William III c. 30)

(i) Newcomers with certificates can be removed only when chargeable.

(ii) Those receiving relief to wear badges.

(iii) Fines for those refusing to take pauper apprentices.

1714 *For Reducing the Laws relating to Rogues . . . and Vagrants into one Act . . .* (13 Anne c. 26)

(i) Constables may remove idle and disorderly beggars, and whip them if recalcitrant. JPs to examine other vagabonds and sessions deal with dangerous and incorrigible rogues: each may order a whipping or hard labour in houses of correction. Rewards for those apprehending them.

(ii) Certain categories of vagrant may be bound to service for seven years, at home or overseas.

(iii) County rates to be levied for the expense of passing vagrants.

* 1723 *For Amending the Laws relating to the Settlement, Employment and Relief of the Poor* [Workhouse Test Act] (9 Geo. I c. 7)

(i) No additions to relief lists unless evidence taken on oath by a JP.

(ii) Churchwardens and overseers may, with consent of parishioners, hire a house or houses and contract with anyone for the maintenance and setting to work of the poor there.

(iii) Poor refusing to be housed there to be denied relief.

(iv) Two or more parishes may unite, with consent of a JP, for these purposes.

1740 *For amending and enforcing the Laws relating to Rogues Vagabonds and other idle and disorderly Persons* . . . (13 Geo. II c. 24)

(i) 'Idle and disorderly', now further defined, may be sent to house of correction for a month's hard labour by a JP.

(ii) JPs to examine vagabonds and pass them home via houses of correction, or send to house of correction until sessions.

(iii) Sessions to sentence incorrigible rogues to up to six months hard labour in houses of correction where they can be whipped.

1744 *To oblige Overseers of the Poor to give public Notice of Rates* . . . (17 Geo. II c. 3)

Notice to be given in church and rates to be available for inspection.

1744 *To amend and make more effectual the Laws relating to Rogues, Vagabonds* . . . (17 Geo. II c. 5)

As 1740, but maximum terms of hard labour increased, JPs may again order ordinary vagabonds to be whipped, and less insistence on passing via houses of correction.

1748 to 1785 Many Local Acts for Poor Relief, including 14 incorporations of parishes in Norfolk and Suffolk 1756–85, the first for the hundreds of Carlford and Colneis, Suffolk (29 Geo. II c. 79): JPs and chief residents to be 'Guardians', appointing 'Directors of the Poor' and 'Acting Guardians' to supervise overseers and levy rates up to maximum of previous 7 years.

* 1782 *For the better Relief and Employment of the Poor* [Gilbert's Act] (22 Geog. III c. 83)

(i) Parishes may unite and nominate Guardians of the Poor, to be appointed by two JPs, salaried and incorporated. A Visitor to supervise them and the Governor of the poor house.

(ii) Overseers in such parishes only to collect rates.

(iii) Only the impotent to go to the poor house; Guardians to maintain and provide for the able-bodied poor elsewhere, hire them out to labour, and make up any deficiency in wages.

(iv) Any JP may order outdoor relief, or order Guardians to provide housing or find employment, for a complainant.

Notes

1. Particularly by the work in progress by Joanna Innes. I am grateful to her for discussing the problems of the eighteenth century with me. See also [Innes, 1990; 1987; Snell, 1985].

2. M. Hale, *A Discourse Touching Provision for the Poor* (1683), pp. 2–3.

3. D. Wilkins, *Concilia* (1737), III, p. 790. I owe this reference to Barbara Harvey.

4. Cf. M. Spufford, 'Puritanism and Social Control?', in A. Fletcher and J. Stevenson (eds), *Order and Disorder in Early Modern England* (Cambridge, 1985), pp. 41–57.

5. B. W. Quintrell (ed.), *Proceedings of the Lancashire Justices of the Peace at the Sheriff's Table during Assizes Week, 1578–1694* (Lancashire and Cheshire Record Society, 121, 1981), pp. 41, 172–7.

6. Bodleian Library, MS. Carte 117, ff. 338–9; Hereford and Worcester Record Office, 746. BA2872.

7. S. A. Peyton (ed.), *Minutes of Proceedings in Quarter Sessions*, I (Lincoln Record Society, 25, 1931), pp. lvi–lvii, xcvii–c.

8. I owe this information to Joanna Innes.

9. Calculations based on the data in P. K. O'Brien, 'The political economy of British taxation, 1660–1815', *Economic History Review*, 2nd ser., 41 (1988), 9. Cf. P. Mathias, *The Transformation of England* (1979), p. 117.

10. R. Burn, *The History of the Poor Laws* (1764), p. 106.

11. The workhouse movement is fully discussed in T. V. Hitchcock, 'The English Workhouse. A Study in Institutional Poor Relief in Selected Counties 1696–1750', unpublished DPhil thesis, Oxford University, 1985.

12. C. Parfect, *Proposals made in the year 1720 to the Parishioners of Stroud . . .* (1729), p. 11.

13. There is as yet no proper study of Gilbert. See his works: *A Scheme for the better Relief and Employment of the Poor*

65

(1764); *A Bill intended to be offered to Parliament* (1775); *Observations upon the Orders and Resolutions of the House* (1775); *Plan for the better Relief and Employment of the Poor* (1781). Cf. R. Burn, *Observations on the Bill* (1776).

14. *An Account of Several Workhouses* (1732), p. iii.

15. T. Gilbert, *Considerations on the Bills for the better Relief and Employment of the Poor* (1787), p. 5; idem, *A Bill* (1786); idem, *A Plan of Police* (1786), pp. 32–3.

16. J. Townsend, *A Dissertation on the Poor Laws* (1786; new edition, Berkeley, 1971), pp. 64, 69.

17. I owe much of the argument at this point to discussions with Richard Smith.

Select Bibliography

Unless otherwise stated, the place of publication of books is London.

GENERAL SURVEYS

A. L. Beier, *The Problem of the Poor in Tudor and Stuart England* (1983). A concise short introduction.

E. M. Leonard, *The Early History of English Poor Relief* (Cambridge, 1900). Still the most thorough account of the period before 1640, but its arguments should be treated sceptically.

D. Marshall, *The English Poor in the Eighteenth Century* (1926). Usefully complements [S. and B. Webb, 1927].

G. Nicholls, *A History of the English Poor Law*, 2 vols (1854). Remains useful for information on eighteenth-century public policy.

G. W. Oxley, *Poor Relief in England and Wales 1601–1834* (1974). A clear guide, especially for the eighteenth century, with full bibliography.

J. Pound, *Poverty and Vagrancy in Tudor England* (1971). A brief survey, with illustrative documents.

P. Slack, *Poverty and Policy in Tudor and Stuart England* (1988). A synthesis of work on the period up to 1712.

G. Taylor, *The Problem of Poverty 1660–1834* (1969). A brief account, with illustrative documents.

S. and B. Webb, *English Poor Law History: Part I. The Old Poor Law* (1927). The classic history for the period after 1688.

A. B. Appleby, *Famine in Tudor and Stuart England* (Liverpool, 1978). Shows the effects of dearth in the north-west.

T. Arkell, 'The incidence of poverty in England in the later seventeenth century', *Social History*, 12 (1987). Interesting on contemporary definitions as well as realities.

R. M. Smith, 'The structured dependence of the elderly as a recent development: some sceptical historical thoughts', *Ageing and Society*, 4 (1984). Valuable for its long chronological perspective.

K. D. M. Snell, *Annals of the Labouring Poor. Social Change in Agrarian England 1660–1900* (Cambridge, 1985). Imaginative use of settlement records to throw new light on labourers.

J. Thirsk (ed.), *The Agrarian History of England and Wales*, vol. IV *1500–1640*, vol. V, parts i and ii, *1640–1750* (Cambridge, 1967, 1985). The standard work on rural society and economic change.

D. Thomson, 'Welfare and the historians', in L. Bonfield, R. M. Smith and K. Wrightson (eds), *The World We Have Gained. Essays presented to Peter Laslett* (Oxford, 1986). Comparable to [Smith, 1984] in reviewing the history of welfare from the point of view of family history.

T. Wales, 'Poverty, poor relief and the life-cycle: some evidence from seventeenth-century Norfolk', in R. M. Smith (ed.), *Land, Kinship and Life-cycle* (Cambridge, 1984). Of more than local importance on the quality of poverty and functions of poor relief in the later seventeenth century.

E. A. Wrigley and R. S. Schofield, *The Population History of England 1541–1871. A Reconstruction* (1981). The authoritative account of the demographic background.

PUBLIC ATTITUDES

J. O. Appleby, *Economic Thought and Ideology in Seventeenth-Century England* (Princeton, 1978). Sets ideas about the poor in the context of economic thought generally.

A. W. Coats, 'Economic thought and poor law policy in the eighteenth century', *Economic History Review*, 2nd ser., 13 (1960). A wide-ranging and influential discussion of public attitudes.

A. W. Coats, 'The relief of poverty, attitudes to labour and economic change in England 1660–1782', *International Review of Social History*, 21 (1976). Expands on [Coats, 1960].

G. Himmelfarb, *The Idea of Poverty. England in the Early Industrial Age* (1984). Includes full discussion of attitudes in the later eighteenth century.

M. Rubin, *Charity and Community in Medieval Cambridge* (Cambridge, 1987). Useful for the medieval background to the poor law.

J. Thirsk, *Economic Policy and Projects. The Development of a Consumer Society in Early Modern England* (Oxford, 1978). Important for its discussion of the economic attitudes and policies behind early projects for the poor.

B. Tierney, *Medieval Poor-Law: A Sketch of Canonical Theory and its Application in England* (Berkeley, 1959). Reveals similarities between medieval and early modern attitudes.

M. Todd, *Christian Humanism and the Puritan Social Order* (Cambridge, 1987). Stresses the humanist contribution to later social attitudes.

C. Webster, *The Great Instauration. Science, Medicine and Reform 1626–1660* (1975). Chapters 4 and 5 describe Interregnum projects for the poor.

POLICY AND LEGISLATION

C. S. L. Davies, 'Slavery and Protector Somerset: The Vagrancy Act of 1547', *Economic History Review*, 2nd ser., 19 (1966). Explores the origins and effects of this eccentric statute.

G. R. Elton, 'An early Tudor poor law', in G. R. Elton, *Studies in Tudor and Stuart Politics and Government*, vol. ii (Cambridge, 1974). Classic account of the 1536 statute.

G. R. Elton, *The Parliament of England 1559–1581* (Cambridge, 1986). Analyses the legislative process, including poor laws.

J. Innes, 'Parliament and the shaping of eighteenth-century

English social policy', *Transactions of the Royal Historical Society*, 5th ser., 40 (1990). Argues that Parliament was more effective as a policy-making body than the Webbs and others have supposed.

B. W. Quintrell, 'The Making of Charles I's Book of Orders', *English Historical Review*, 95 (1980). Sets the Book in the context of earlier developments.

M. Ransome, 'The parliamentary career of Sir Humphrey Mackworth 1701–13', *University of Birmingham Historical Journal*, 1 (1948). On an early attempt to reform the poor law.

P. Slack, 'Books of Orders: The making of English social policy, 1577–1631', *Transactions of the Royal Historical Society*, 5th ser., 30 (1980). Complements [Quintrell, 1980] by looking at other books of orders.

THE MACHINERY OF GOVERNMENT

I. R. Christie, *Stress and Stability in Late Eighteenth-Century Britain* (Oxford, 1984). Chapter IV assesses the contribution of the poor law to political stability.

A. Fletcher, *Reform in the Provinces. The Government of Stuart England* (New Haven, 1986). Chapter 7 draws together a large body of material on the local enforcement of the poor laws.

J. Innes, 'Prisons for the Poor: English Bridewells 1555–1800', in F. Snyder and D. Hay (eds), *Labour, Law and Crime. An historical perspective* (1987). Describes the local adoption of houses of correction, and their implications for policy.

J. R. Kent, *The English Village Constable 1580–1642* (Oxford, 1986). The fullest discussion of the lowest level of local government.

N. Landau, *The Justices of the Peace 1679–1760* (Berkeley, 1984). Particularly interesting on justices' activity outside quarter sessions.

M. K. McIntosh, 'Local responses to the poor in late medieval and Tudor England', *Continuity and Change*, 3 (1988). Useful for developments before the poor law.

S. Wright (ed.), *Parish, Church and People. Local Studies in Lay Religion 1350–1750* (1988). Essays throwing new light on the role of the parish in social welfare at different periods.

MOBILITY AND SETTLEMENT

A. L. Beier, *Masterless Men. The Vagrancy Problem in England 1560–1640* (1985). The fullest and most reliable account of the subject.

P. Clark and D. Souden (eds), *Migration and Society in Early Modern England* (1987). Includes important essays on the seventeenth and eighteenth centuries.

N. Landau, 'The laws of settlement and the surveillance of immigration in eighteenth-century Kent', *Continuity and Change*, 3 (1988). Shows how local authorities discriminated in their use of the law.

P. Styles, 'The Evolution of the Law of Settlement', in P. Styles, *Studies in Seventeenth-Century West Midlands History* (Kineton, 1978). The best account of the complexities of the law.

J. S. Taylor, 'The Impact of Pauper Settlement 1691–1834', *Past and Present*, 73 (1976). A thorough discussion of the law's effects.

PUBLIC HEALTH AND MEDICAL CARE

M. Pelling, 'Healing the Sick Poor: Social Policy and Disability in Norwich 1550–1640', *Medical History*, 29 (1985).

M. Pelling, 'Illness among the poor in an early modern town: the Norwich census of 1570', *Continuity and Change*, 3 (1988). Shows how widespread disability was.

P. Slack, *The Impact of Plague in Tudor and Stuart England* (1985). Describes the effects of epidemics and the policies adopted to combat them.

E. G. Thomas, 'The Old Poor Law and Medicine', *Medical History*, 24 (1980). On medical aid under the poor law in the eighteenth century.

J. Woodward, *To Do The Sick No Harm. A Study of the British Voluntary Hospital System to 1875* (1974). Discusses the new hospitals of the eighteenth century.

CHARITY AND PHILANTHROPY

W. G. Bittle and R. T. Lane, 'Inflation and Philanthropy in England: A Re-Assessment of W. K. Jordan's Data', *Economic History Review*, 2nd ser., 29 (1976). Critical of [Jordan, 1959] but should be read with [Hadwin, 1978].

S. Brigden, 'Religion and Social Obligation in Early Sixteenth-Century London', *Past and Present*, 103 (1984). A valuable discussion of charity in theory and practice.

P. Clark, *Sociability and Urbanity: Clubs and Societies in the Eighteenth Century City* (Dyos Memorial Lecture, Leicester, 1988). Points to the importance of friendly societies.

J. F. Hadwin, 'Deflating Philanthropy', *Economic History Review*, 2nd ser., 31 (1978). An important reworking of the figures in [Jordan, 1959].

W. K. Jordan, *Philanthropy in England 1480–1660* (1959). Summarises exhaustive research on wills, also described in further volumes, including [Jordan, 1960].

W. K. Jordan, *The Charities of London 1480–1660* (1960).

R. K. McClure, *Coram's Children: The London Foundling Hospital in the Eighteenth Century* (New Haven, 1981).

S. Nash, 'Prostitution and Charity: The Magdalen Hospital, A Case Study', *Journal of Social History* 17 (1984). Discusses the origins and purposes of a mid-eighteenth century charity.

D. Owen, *English Philanthropy 1660–1960* (Cambridge, Mass., 1964). A rounded and clear account of eighteenth century developments.

J. S. Taylor, *Jonas Hanway. Founder of the Marine Society* (1985). A life of the leading publicist for philanthropy in the mid-eighteenth century.

C. Wilson, 'Poverty and Philanthropy in Early Modern England', in T. Riis (ed.), *Aspects of Poverty in Early Modern Europe* (Florence:

European University Institute, 1981). Valuable especially for the eighteenth century.

LOCAL STUDIES: BEFORE c 1700

A. L. Beier, 'Poor Relief in Warwickshire 1630–60', *Past and Present*, 35 (1966). Shows the continuity of policy across the Civil War period.

A. L. Beier, 'The social problems of an Elizabethan country town: Warwick 1580–90', in P. Clark (ed.), *Country Towns in Pre-industrial England* (Leicester, 1981).

W. Newman Brown, 'The receipt of poor relief and family situation: Aldenham, Hertfordshire 1630–90', in Smith (ed.), *Land, Kinship and Life-cycle* (see [Wales, 1984]).

F. G. Emmison, 'Poor-relief Accounts of two rural Parishes in Bedfordshire 1563–98', *Economic History Review*, 3 (1931).

F. G. Emmison, 'The Care of the Poor in Elizabethan Essex', *Essex Review*, 62 (1953).

E. M. Hampson, *The Treatment of Poverty in Cambridgeshire 1597–1834* (Cambridge, 1934). One of the earliest and best local studies.

S. Macfarlane, 'Social policy and the poor in the later seventeenth century', in A. L. Beier and R. Finlay (eds), *London 1500–1700: The Making of the Metropolis* (1986). Examines the revival of the London Corporation of the Poor in the 1690s.

V. Pearl, 'Puritans and Poor Relief: The London Workhouse 1649–1660', in D. Pennington and K. Thomas (eds), *Puritans and Revolutionaries. Essays presented to Christopher Hill* (Oxford, 1978). Discusses the first London Corporation of the Poor of the Interregnum.

V. Pearl. 'Social Policy in Early Modern London', in H. Lloyd-Jones, V. Pearl and B. Worden ceds), *History and Imagination. Essays in honour of H. R. Trevor-Roper* (1981). A rounded account of poor relief in seventeenth century London.

J. F. Pound, 'An Elizabethan Census of the Poor', *University of Birmingham Historical Journal*, 8 (1962). On the reforms of 1570 in Norwich.

P. Slack, 'Poverty and Politics in Salisbury 1597–1666', in P. Clark and P. Slack (eds), *Crisis and Order in English Towns*

73

1500–1700 (1972). Describes municipal projects initiated by Puritans.

LOCAL STUDIES: AFTER *c.* 1700

P. Anderson, 'The Leeds Workhouse under the Old Poor Law 1726–1834', *Thoresby Miscellany XVII* (Thoresby Society, 56, 1981).

A. W. Ashby, 'One Hundred Years of Poor Law Administration in a Warwickshire Village', *Oxford Studies in Social and Legal History*, vol. III (Oxford, 1912). A detailed study of eighteenth century Tysoe.

W. L. Blease, 'The Poor Law in Liverpool 1681–1834', *Transactions of the Lancashire and Cheshire Historical Society*, 61 (1909).

J. S. Cockburn, 'The North Riding Justices, 1690–1750. A Study in Local Administration', *Yorkshire Archaeological Journal*, 41 (1963–6). Interesting on vagrancy.

A. Digby, *Pauper Palaces* (1978). On nineteenth century Norfolk, but early chapters are valuable for developments before 1800.

A. H. Dodd, 'The Old Poor Law in North Wales', *Archaeologia Cambrensis*, 7th ser., 6 (1926). Shows the slow implementation of the law.

G. C. Edmonds, 'Accounts of Eighteenth-Century Overseers of the Poor of Chalfont St Peter', *Records of Buckinghamshire*, 18 (1966).

F. G. Emmison, *The Relief of the Poor at Eaton Socon 1706–1834* (Bedfordshire Historical Record Society, 15, 1933).

H. Fearn, 'The Financing of the Poor-Law Incorporation for the Hundreds of Colneis and Carlford in the County of Suffolk, 1758–1820', *Proceedings of the Suffolk Institute of Archaeology*, 27 (1958). Material on the first incorporated hundreds in East Anglia.

R. P. Hastings, *Poverty and the Poor Law in the North Riding of Yorkshire c. 1780–1837* (York: Borthwick Paper 61, 1982).

G. B. Hindle (ed.), *Provision for the Relief of the Poor in Manchester 1754–1826* (Chetham Society, 3rd ser., 22, 1975).

F. H. Hinton, 'Notes on the Administration of the Relief of the Poor of Lacock 1583 to 1834', *Wiltshire Archaeological Magazine*, 49 (1940–2).

G. Jackson, *Hull in the Eighteenth Century* (Oxford, 1972). Contains interesting material on charity and poor relief.

G. W. Oxley, 'The Permanent Poor in South-West Lanchashire under the Old Poor Law', in J. R. Harris (ed.), *Liverpool and Merseyside* (1969). One of the best modern studies of an important locality.

P. Ripley, 'Poverty in Gloucester and its Alleviation 1690–1740', *Transactions of the Bristol and Gloucestershire Archaeological Society*, 103 (1985).

THE END OF THE OLD POOR LAW 1782–1834

M. Blaug, 'The Myth of the Old Poor Law and the Making of the New', *Journal of Economic History*, 23 (1963). A seminal paper defending the Old Poor Law against its critics.

G. R. Boyer, 'The Old Poor Law and the Agricultural Labour Market in Southern England: An Empirical Analysis', *Journal of Economic History*, 46 (1986).

J. P. Huzel, 'Malthus, the Poor Law, and Population in Early Nineteenth-Century England', *Economic History Review* 2nd ser., 22 (1969).

P. Mandler, 'The Making of the New Poor Law *Redivivus*', *Past and Present*, 117 (1987), followed by debate in *Past and Present*, 127 (1990). Mandler argues, against his critics, that changing attitudes among the landed gentry paved the way for the New Poor Law.

J. D. Marshall, *The Old Poor Law 1795–1834* (1968, new edition 1985). Excellent short guide to the historical controversies.

J. R. Poynter, *Society and Pauperism, English Ideas on Poor Relief 1795–1834* (1969). The best account of contemporary debates.

K. Williams, *From Pauperism to Poverty* (1981). Reassesses, and criticises, some of the conclusions in [Blaug, 1963].

OTHER COUNTRIES

C. Lis and H. Soly, *Poverty and Capitalism in Pre-industrial Europe* (Hassocks, 1979). Useful on sixteenth century innovations.

75

R. Mitchison, 'The Making of the Old Scottish Poor Law', *Past and Present*, 63 (1974). Explains why implementation of the law was slow in Scotland.

B. Pullan, 'Catholics and the Poor in Early Modern Europe', *Transactions of the Royal Historical Society*, 5th ser., 26 (1976). Shows both similarities and contrasts with Protestant countries.

B. Pullan, 'Support and redeem: charity and poor relief in Italian cities from the fourteenth to the seventeenth century', *Continuity and Change*, 3 (1988). Supplements [Pullan, 1976].

SOME PRINTED SOURCES

S. G. and E. O. A. Checkland (eds), *The Poor Law Report of 1834* (1974). Tendentious, critical and informative about the Old Poor Law.

G. Clarke (ed.), *John Bellers. His Life, Times and Writings* (1987). A late seventeenth century Quaker philanthropist and projector.

F. M. Eden, *The State of the Poor*, 3 vols (1797). A classic collection of material. (Abridged edition, by A. G. L. Rogers, 1928.)

T. V. Hitchcock (ed.), *Richard Hutton's Complaints Book* (London Record Society, 24, 1987). Notebook of the steward of the Quaker workhouse in Clerkenwell, London, 1711–37, with a useful introduction.

E. Melling (ed.), *Kentish Sources: IV. The Poor* (Maidstone, 1964).

J. F. Pound (ed.), *The Norwich Census of the Poor 1570* (Norfolk Record Society, 40, 1971). The most thorough of the early listings of the poor.

P. Slack (ed.), *Poverty in Early-Stuart Salisbury* (Wiltshire Record Society, 31, 1975).

D. Vaisey (ed.), *The Diary of Thomas Turner 1754–1765* (Oxford, 1984). Turner was, among other things, overseer of the poor.

J. Webb (ed.), *Poor Relief in Elizabethan Ipswich* (Suffolk Records Society, 9, 1966).

Index

Jordan, W.K., 50, 52
justices of the peace, 56; activities, 28, 45–6; legal powers, 18–19, 36, 39, 59–64 *passim*; vested interests, 46–8

labouring poor, 12, 27, 28, 33, 53, 54
Lancashire, 47
Leeds, 42, 47, 52
Liverpool, 42
local government, 48; *see also* parishes
Locke, John, 41
London, 12, 15–16, 19, 44, 50; Corporation of the Poor, 25, 45, 46, 61–2; hospitals, 16, 24, 51
Lyons, 14

Mackworth, Sir Humphrey, 41
Malthus, Thomas, 54, 55
Manchester, 52
Mandeville, Bernard, 44
Marine Society, 51
Marryott, Matthew, 41
Marshall, William, 15, 17
Massie, Joseph, 51
migration, 36–9
Montagu, Henry, earl of Manchester, 23

Nacton, Suff., 43
national income, 30, 33
Nelson, Robert, 51
Norfolk, 43, 63
Northamptonshire, 23
Norwich, 19–20, 24, 32, 41

Olney, Bucks, 41
overseers, 27–9, 40, 56, 60, 61, 63; attempts to control, 45–7
Oxford, 15
Oxfordshire, 19

parishes, 26–9, 36–9; civil, 18, 57–8; powers of, 19, 59–62;

unions of, 41–2, 45, 47, 63, 64
Parliament, 17, 19–21, 35, 47–8, 56–7; inquiries into poor relief, 30, 52; *see also* poor law
party politics, 46, 57
patriotism, 51
philanthropy, 44, 49–52, 53; 'associated', 50–1, 52; *see also* charity
plague, 15, 22, 61
poor, attitudes of, 13, 22, 29, 38, 44, 52, 56; *see also* poverty
poor law; development of, 17–21; local Acts, 43, 45, 48; medieval, 13; reform of, 35–48 *passim*; statutes summarised, 59–64; 1598 Relief Act, 18–19, 60–1; 1662 Settlement Act, 36, 62; 1723 Workhouse Test Act, 40–2, 45, 47, 63; 1782 Gilbert's Act, 43–4, 47–8, 63–4; 1832 Commission, 46, 54; 1834 Amendment Act, 45, 48
poor rates, 18, 19, 20–1, 60–4 *passim*; amounts raised by, 26, 29–34, 53; character of recipients, 27–8, 53–6; 'in aid', 45; method of raising, 28; numbers relieved by, 33–4; spread of, 26; *see also* overseers

population: age-structure of, 32–3; declining, 42; family structure of, 13–14, 55; pressure, 11, 12, 24, 29, 31, 33, 50, 54
poverty: causes of, 11–14, 53–4; definitions of, 12, 13, 14, 33, 55–6
prostitutes, 51
Protestantism, 11, 14, 16
Puritanism, 11, 20, 24–5

Quakers, 46, 50

rate-payers, 34
Reading, 42